LESSONS FROM THE

EASTERN
WARRIORS

Fred Neff

**Photographs by James Reid
and Patrick O'Leary**

Lerner Publications Company • Minneapolis

To my father, Elliot Neff, and my mother, Mollie Neff, whose enthusiasm for knowledge and interest in continuing education has been an inspiration for me.

The models photographed in this book are Christa Neff, Richard DeValerio, Jim Reid, William McLeod, Elias Murdock, Helena Koudelka, and Peter Koudelka.

Japanese calligraphy on back cover by Kenichi Tazawa.

Library of Congress Cataloging-in-Publication Data
Neff, Fred.
   Lessons from the Eastern warriors : dynamic self-defense
techniques / by Fred Neff ; photographs by James Reid and Patrick
O'Leary.
     p. cm.
   Includes index.
   ISBN 0-8225-1166-5
   1. Self-defense. 2. Martial arts. I. Title.
GV1111.N452 1993
613.6'6—dc20   92-37937
                                       CIP

Manufactured in the United States of America
1 2 3 4 5 6 – I/SF – 99 98 97 96 95 94

CONTENTS

1 Introduction / 5

2 History / 7

3 Basic Philosophy / 11

4 Common Questions / 18

5 Physical Conditioning / 21

6 Fighting Postures and Movement / 29

7 Sensitive Areas on the Body / 41

8 Safety-Range and Long-Range Defenses / 43

9 Close-Range Defenses / 73

10 Grappling and Wrestling / 85

11 Strategy / 101

12 Safety Considerations / 109

Index / 111

CHAPTER
1

INTRODUCTION

In the West, we generally think of warriors as soldiers who fight for their country out of loyalty and, perhaps, for glory and conquest. A special type of warrior, however—one who trains to promote health, spiritual and philosophical growth, self-improvement, and harmony with nature—has been traditional in the Orient. These Eastern Warriors develop skill in combat as part of their overall development as a person. They use fighting only to defend themselves and to protect society's best interests. Furthermore, they fight according to the rules of an Asian empty-hand system: their bodies are their weapons.

Geographic origin is less important than one's fighting style. An ordinary soldier would not be considered an Eastern Warrior simply because he or she was from Asia, and a person from the West who regularly practices an Eastern martial art may be considered an Eastern Warrior.

To better understand how the different types of warriors developed, one must look back in history. In the West, the ancient Mesopotamians, Egyptians, Greeks, and Persians used soldiers to conquer or defend territory. Soldiers learned to use weapons, and, as hand-to-hand combat became less important in battle, people skilled in the art of weaponless fighting gradually began to use

5

their techniques for sport. The Greeks contributed greatly to this separation between soldier and athlete through the development of Olympic contests. Today, we think of the Western fighting arts of wrestling and boxing not as military techniques, but as sports to be practiced by athletes and enjoyed by spectators.

In the East, however, hand-to-hand fighting evolved differently. Eastern religious leaders accepted the idea that the mind, body, and spirit must work together, and they used weaponless fighting techniques to promote physical and spiritual health and to defend themselves. These ancient practitioners of martial arts were an early type of Eastern Warrior. Over time, they emphasized that martial-arts training could develop the inner self to stand up better to the rigors, pressures, and threats of living. Because other weapons were outlawed, these warriors developed martial arts that emphasized the human body as a fighting instrument. Known as empty-hand warriors, they were able to fight without weapons in an effective and beautiful way. Not just soldiers or athletes, they strove to bring their minds, bodies, and spirits together.

The techniques they developed are still valuable in coping with the great stress and danger of modern life. This book draws on lessons taught by the Eastern Warriors from a variety of East Asian fighting traditions. The core techniques, however, are from modern *kempo,* meaning "fist way." Kempo derives from the Chinese art of *Chuan-Fa,* also meaning "fist way," which was brought to Japan by Chinese visitors and blended with native forms of *ju-jutsu,* meaning "gentle art." This combination became, over time, the separate art of kempo.

The road to becoming an effective Eastern Warrior is enjoyable if you are patient and allow yourself to improve over time in all aspects of the training. This book should not be your only source of knowledge about self-defense. Instead, it can introduce you to the martial arts of the Eastern Warriors and supplement the training offered by a qualified instructor. You may—with diligent practice and study of the Eastern Warriors' fighting forms and philosophy—achieve numerous benefits, including better health, a stronger body, skill in self-defense, greater self-confidence, and harmony with others.

CHAPTER

2

HISTORY

Thirteenth century Japanese scroll depicting the "Burning of the Sanjo Palace"

The martial arts of the Eastern Warriors can be traced from very early times to the present. In China, evidence of the use of fighting arts—including both hand-to-hand and weapon-based methods—dates back to almost the dawn of civilization. One strategist, Sun-Tzu, who lived more than 2,000 years ago, wrote *The Art of War,* a book that is still considered a valuable guide to dealing with conflict and competition.

The Chinese were not the only contributors to the fighting arts of Eastern Warriors. Persian warriors, known for their tremendous sense of rhythm and timing combined with expert grappling, were masters of hand-to-hand combat. In the fourth century B.C., the Greeks under Alexander the Great taught the

Persians calisthenics as well as fighting techniques from the Greek art of *pankration.* This art included punching, kicking, throwing, choking, headbutting, joint locks, and grappling. These fighting techniques of the Persians and the Greeks eventually made their way to India, the great crossroads of trade between the East and the West.

Indian warriors already had their own established fighting arts, but Indian combat systems began to add techniques brought by the Persians and the Greeks. As a result, martial skill developed tremendously among Indian warriors and caravan guards. One of the more effective fighting arts in India—one that is still practiced—is *Kalaripayit,* which is similar in many ways to certain forms of

A Samurai's armor, made in the early 1800s

Chinese *Kung-Fu*. This resemblance may not be coincidental, since both Indian religious leaders and caravan guards brought Buddhist philosophy and fighting techniques eastward into China.

On the Chinese mainland, various fighting techniques known to ancient cultures combined and blossomed into the effective martial arts associated with the Eastern Warriors. Just who first brought techniques from India into China is unknown, but some historians have dated the transmission of these fighting forms to China from the legend of the great Buddhist monk Ta Mo, also called Daruma or Bodhidharma.

Sometime between A.D. 516 and 528, the learned Ta Mo probably brought Indian philosophy and physical health practices to the Shaolin temple in China. Some scholars have even argued that this was the beginning of the fighting arts in China, but that is an exaggeration. The Chinese had already developed sophisticated fighting forms and strategies of their own.

What Ta Mo *did* introduce was a unique philosophy called *Chan*—which is similar to what is commonly known as Zen Buddhism—along with certain key health practices. Chan, as taught by Ta Mo, included meditation and development of the inner self to be in tune with nature and its ways. Ta Mo's original goal was to teach this high form of philosophy along with health practices and *not* fighting arts. The physical exercises first introduced by Ta Mo were probably intended to maintain the monks' physical health so they could better endure the challenges of living. Ta Mo himself was originally from a warrior caste in India, so he was almost certainly familiar with empty-hand fighting techniques. The exercises that he taught were probably little more than an outline of fighting techniques.

After Ta Mo left the temple, his students may have elaborated upon the exercises he first introduced. His original art probably taught a set of 18 actions to be done regularly in the morning. He has also been credited with writing the great Chinese masterpiece known as the *I Chin Ching,* or Muscle-Change Classic, which sets forth key movements for health.

It was precisely this unification of philosophy and physical techniques that brought fame to the monks of the Shaolin temple. They traveled from the temple, demonstrating their skills to amazed viewers. Some monks even taught outsiders certain fighting skills.

After a number of years, these students developed their own martial arts, which combined various fighting techniques and were classified as being either internal or external boxing systems.

Internal systems relied upon the development of proper form, breath control, balance, and mind power. The external systems relied instead upon great physical strength, developed through body conditioning, and the effective use of body mechanics to deliver power. These two early forms of fighting were referred to as Chuan-Fa. Some people—impressed by the great knowledge of Shaolin monks in fighting and in other important disciplines—also called these arts *Kung-Fu,* meaning "learned man."

These Kung-Fu techniques were eventually systematized by key persons such as Ch'ueh Yuan, also called Kiao Yuan. He has been credited with refining the Shaolin system of fighting to embrace 72 fighting forms. Still later, more forms were added to develop a pool of 170 fighting forms. Some historians believe that Ch'ueh Yuan worked with one or more other martial-arts masters to create the pool, which is the foundation for many of the modern schools of Shaolin.

As the 170 forms were developed, they were divided into five styles known as the dragon, tiger, leopard, snake, and crane. Each animal had one significant essence that was important to the martial artist. The dragon helped the person develop great power of spirit; the tiger, bone power; the leopard, extreme strength. The snake taught warriors to bring out the great internal power of *ch'i,* the vital life force in all things. The crane taught sinew training, which takes its name from the solid, resilient strength seen in cord or thread. When these essences combine in one fighting technique, it includes both internal and external power and gives the ability to harness mind, body, and spirit for defense or other purposes. Later students of martial arts did not always master all five essences, but instead concentrated on one or two particular methods of fighting. They in turn developed different schools of fighting of their own.

By the beginning of the 20th century, styles of fighting differed tremendously in techniques and general emphasis on self-defense. The various styles are usually classified as either northern or southern Chuan-Fa, depending on whether they were more common north or south of China's Yangtze River. In general, the northern schools emphasize more long-range techniques such as punching and kicking, with a concentration on the development of external power. Southern styles stress close-range fighting, shorter punches, holds, balance, and a concentration on harnessing inner power that is characteristic of an internal system. Defining a school as northern or southern is based on general differences rather than absolutes. Some schools aren't easily classified because they blend techniques from both northern and southern schools.

Chinese martial arts have proven extremely effective in developing a person's health and fighting ability. Other people have adapted Chinese ways and learned from them. The inhabitants of Okinawa, an island between China and Japan, blended their native fighting techniques with styles from China to create what we know today as *karate,* which means "empty hand."

Karate makes an empty-hand warrior equal in power to a far bigger individual. In Japan, Chuan-Fa techniques blended with sophisticated native grappling and locking techniques to create early versions of the art of kempo. Kempo techniques are thus very similar to certain Kung-Fu or Chuan-Fa styles and techniques. It is important, however, to understand that kempo is unique and stands apart from the Chinese arts of Chuan-Fa and Kung-Fu. Modern kempo systems combine Chinese fighting techniques, Japanese ju-jutsu, and fighting tactics from other countries.

Although the various empty-hand self-defense systems have distinctive techniques and emphases, they share a foundation in the history of Asian fighting arts. A person who practices such forms of ancient physical culture and self-defense is the modern counterpart of an ancient Eastern Warrior. The ancient warriors trained mind, body, and spirit to work together to develop character, virtue, and strength. Out of this training, a person can learn to handle the inner foes of worry, anxiety, and self-doubt, as well as outside forces, such as a strong adversary whose aggression must be contained.

3

BASIC PHILOSOPHY

A bronze statue of Buddha

Philosophy is an integral part of the Asian martial arts practiced by the Eastern Warriors. Despite differences in thought and emphasis, most Asian fighting systems share common philosophic beliefs and practices from various sources. Eastern Warriors blended the philosophy of the *Tao,* the yin-yang concept, Chan (or Zen) Buddhism, and Confucianism. Each of these teachings plays a part in developing the basic ethics, beliefs, and practices shared by many Asian martial arts.

THE TAO

The ancient Chinese philosopher Lao-Tzu popularized the concept of the Tao (dow), which means "the way." He explained that all the universe was affected by Tao, an external force of tremendous power. A person who realizes and follows the Tao will reach enlightenment and find happiness and fulfillment.

Lao-Tzu taught that to understand the Tao, people must first see the opposite of what

11

Heavily etched rock formations alongside China's Yangtze River

they seek and acknowledge its presence. For example, someone who seeks strength must first admit weakness. Lao-Tzu also taught that people who are honest and act sincerely gain contentment. Such people are free to be modest and show compassion without concern for what others may think. Their humility and kindness show that they are secure and do not need to brag or harm others. Individuals unschooled in the Tao may interpret such actions as weakness, but the Tao teaches that such weakness is really strength.

It was important to Lao-Tzu that people learn to be content with their place in nature, thus avoiding the extremes of conduct that cause great problems in the natural world. For example, extreme rains lead to floods, while an extreme shortage of rain leads to drought. Drawing a lesson from nature, Lao-Tzu taught that people must not go too far in any direction. When people live moderately, they can be in harmony with nature. Lao-Tzu insisted that people should do nothing artificial. This concept can have far-reaching effects. Through simple living and following nature's ways, people develop power and virtue, elements that the Eastern Warriors aim to achieve.

YIN-YANG

The ancient Chinese yin-yang concept of nature also contributed to the philosophy of Asian martial arts. According to the yin-yang concept, opposing forces, referred to as the yin and the yang, are built into everything in nature. If people understand the built-in opposing forces, they can take appropriate action to keep the forces in balance. The yang includes those aspects of something that are strong, light, or active; the yin includes those things that are weak, dark, or passive.

The yin-yang concept is represented by the symbol of a circle with a wavy line, similar to an *S*, down the center of it. The wavy line represents the principle of continual movement in and out and up and down within the circle. One side of the circle is dark, while the other side is light, to show the two opposing forces in all of nature. The light area has a dark spot, or eye, representing the yin within it, and the dark area has a light spot representing the yang within it. The spots show that within each side lies the seed of the opposing force. The interaction of yin and yang is the creative force behind what happens in the world. If the forces are out of balance, undesirable events can result.

Eastern Warriors use the yin-yang concept to be more effective in fighting. For example, it can be used to understand how to execute a blow. The arm should be soft or loose until it hits the target and then become hard or rigid to release maximum power. Once the blow has been delivered, the arm returns to its loose or relaxed state. Only by combining the opposing forces of soft and hard can maximum power be achieved. Blending the yin-yang concept with Taoist philosophy created more ways to evaluate and develop effective fighting techniques, tactics, and strategy.

CONFUCIANISM

Confucian philosophy has greatly affected the thinking of people throughout the world. It originated with the teachings of the great Chinese philosopher Confucius, or K'ung-Tzu, as he is commonly known in China, who lived from 551 to 479 B.C. Confucius was concerned with how people relate to each other rather than how they relate to nature. He taught that all relations between people must be based on natural affection, good will, and sympathetic understanding or fairness. Justice, according to Confucius, was not just doing what seems right under the circumstances, but what would lead to a balanced society.

Confucius stressed the development of the superior person, who would only do what was proper and right at any given time. This superior person followed a firm code of ethics and morality. Students of Confucianism patterned themselves on a superior person, often their teacher. Eastern Warriors patterned not only their fighting techniques but also their attitudes and reactions after their teachers.

Confucius also stressed that, to promote peace, order, and harmony in society, people must relate to one another courteously. He taught that each person's desires must be balanced against the needs of others. The superior person finds happiness by achieving this balance and avoiding excesses in conduct. This person, by following certain patterns known as rituals, may also gain great power. This power is not necessarily physical power; it could also be inner contentment and satisfaction. Ultimately, a person may derive power not by seizing it from others but by relating to others properly, acting in the way of a superior person, avoiding excess, and following traditional structures laid down for achievement.

CHAN BUDDHISM

Today we often refer to concepts of Chan Buddhism as Zen, after the Japanese interpretation of them. Chan Buddhism developed out of philosophic concepts brought from India to China by the legendary Ta Mo. What Ta Mo taught at the Shaolin temple in China was eventually named Chan.

Chan teachings developed into several different branches, and many of the Eastern martial arts accepted a form of them. Chan is not a religion but an inner way of handling life. Often when people try too hard to accomplish things, the pressure they put on themselves creates obstacles to achieving their goals. Chan Buddhism emphasizes learning how to react in a natural, open way to such experiences. It accepts that humans have many natural abilities that, if allowed to func-

Chinese warrior statue at the entrance to the tombs of the Ming emperors

tion without interference, can solve both inner and outer problems. Chan Buddhism encourages people to direct their energies to bring out these natural, positive abilities.

Chan also teaches that when people become self-conscious, they often become indecisive and stumble or fail to accomplish what needs to be done. Indecision disrupts the pursuit of solutions. To reach full effectiveness, practitioners learn to develop a pure

14

mind, sometimes referred to as no-mind. A pure mind is open and does not let inner or outer disturbances disrupt it.

The no-mind concept has been compared to a smooth pond. It has no ripple, so it reflects clearly everything near its surface. Chan teaches that when the mind is able to reflect, it can react appropriately to any threat.

This concept appealed to warriors searching for guidance. Followers of Chan are free from excessive worry because they practice something adequately, their minds become free, and they can take effective action. For example, people who look at their feet when walking down steps may stumble. If, however, they do not concern themselves with each step, but move down them naturally, they do not trip or stumble. This type of effortless action is accomplished through acceptance of Chan Buddhism.

PHILOSOPHIC GUIDELINES FROM THE EASTERN WARRIORS

Eastern Warriors strive to allow every act to flow freely and naturally. They learn the techniques of fighting so well that each technique can be done naturally when needed. They do not have to analyze each movement while doing it. Their minds and bodies are free to move through the technique without restriction or fear of failure. They learn to tune out distractions and concentrate on what needs to be done. They gain a feeling of being at one with the techniques they are doing. In this process, the body becomes free from restrictions and tension put there by negative experience or criticism. Because the mind sends no negative signals, the body can move automatically to perform. There is no limit to what an Eastern Warrior can accomplish once self-doubt is driven away.

Over time, the philosophies of the Tao, yin-yang, Confucianism, and Chan Buddhism gradually formed the philosophic basis of East Asian martial arts. The blend included a distinct ethical and moral position that was accepted by many different Asian martial arts.

Most Eastern Warriors try to develop mind, body, and spirit. All people have weak points that they must work on, but weaknesses can be corrected by proper thinking, exercise, practice of martial arts, and experience. The rigor of training for combat also expands an individual's capabilities. The inner challenge of bringing mind, body, and spirit together to achieve a goal leads to self-discovery. This process also teaches people how to handle external challenges such as a hostile adversary. Over time and with proper practice and discipline, practitioners learn how to channel their efforts to reach maximum effectiveness. They also gain awareness of the importance of acting in harmony with all other living things. When people learn to relate properly to others, they find more inner happiness, and they more easily fulfill their goals.

What follows is a breakdown and discussion of the 10 universal guidelines for personal growth in the Eastern Warrior's philosophy.

1. *Follow gradual progress.* Beginning students of martial arts must learn not to move too quickly in their practice and studies. By practicing a little bit each day, the body and mind learn to perform techniques effectively. This lesson goes beyond the fighting arts and is important in everyday living. The East Asian mar-tial arts teach that any creation, whether it is a building or an Eastern Warrior, is only as strong as its foundation. If practitioners put forth quality effort and follow gradual progress to build a strong foundation, they will achieve lasting strength.

2. *Persevere through adversity.* No matter how skillful martial artists are, they will always run into barriers. Sometimes the barriers they face are brought on by their own thoughts or actions. At other times, they are caused by someone else or by external events. Those who persevere will prevail, or at least reach a state of contentment.

3. *Practice moderation.* Eastern Warriors, and all people, face different choices when reacting to a situation. They must decide how much or how little to do. Even a good thing can turn into evil if done to excess. For example, a favorite food eaten in moderate amounts can bring pleasure, while the same food eaten to excess can make you sick. This simple lesson applies to nearly everything a person does in life.

4. *Cultivate a peaceful nature.* Eastern Warriors learn to accept themselves and their role in the world so that they can live in harmony with others and achieve their goals. Constant fighting or strife only interrupt inner contentment and deplete outer strength.

5. *Act in harmony with the environment.* Harmony with the environment was taught by many of the great martial-arts teachers. Each stressed the importance of acting naturally to avoid causing problems for one's self, others, and the en-

vironment. People who observe and follow nature's ways are likely to be happy. Eastern Warriors look on nature as a teacher, and they are never so conceited as to feel they have nothing more to learn.

6. *Act sincerely.* Eastern Warriors must be genuinely sincere in both words and actions. Being sincere and honest makes people feel stronger and more confident, so they can put maximum effort into a project or challenge.

7. *Be fair.* Eastern Warriors must develop a firm belief in and dedication to justice and act accordingly. They should be fair in all their dealings with other people.

8. *Learn self-respect.* Eastern Warriors are encouraged to respect themselves and to find satisfaction in their personal growth.

9. *Use visualization as a tool.* Eastern Warriors learn to form a mental image of themselves performing a task or doing a series of acts. By closing their eyes and imagining themselves doing something well from start to finish, they form a positive mental blueprint for action.

10. *Make a commitment to improvement.* Eastern Warriors learn to continually seek enlightenment and virtue. They improve daily through study in the martial arts, formal schooling, and positive everyday experiences.

CHAPTER

4

COMMON QUESTIONS

1. Are ancient martial arts as effective as modern fighting systems such as karate?

Ancient systems of martial arts share many elements with modern-day karate. The use of formal weapons was, however, a substantial part of these early combat-oriented arts. Many fighting techniques were designed for life-and-death struggles. Modern karate is primarily an empty-hand system of self-defense, with weapons used in some schools as supplementary training instruments. Although karate can be dangerous if misused, many teachers protect against this by teaching techniques appropriate for use in modern self-defense. Both ancient martial arts and modern karate would be extremely effective in a real-life confrontation.

2. Have any secrets of the ancient Eastern Warriors been lost over time?

Distrust and lack of time caused many instructors to not teach certain techniques to their students, but a tremendous pool of fighting methods was still passed down for use. There are so many different techniques that no one could learn more than a fraction of them in his or her lifetime. It is not how many techniques martial-arts practitioners know that makes them effective, but how well they use what they know. Beginning students should concentrate on developing a proper foundation in fundamental techniques.

These techniques are flexible and powerful enough to handle many common self-defense situations.

3. What is the difference between northern and southern schools of Chinese martial arts?

In the past, northern schools generally emphasized long-range punches and kicks that required strong body conditioning. Southern schools used more close-range techniques and emphasized balance, breath control, and mental attitude. Today, both schools use many similar techniques and tactics. It is not unusual to find techniques from different arts blended in a particular style of fighting. For these reasons, one should look at all the major techniques of a particular style before assuming automatically that it will be a northern or southern style just because it originated in a particular part of China.

4. What is meant when someone describes a fighting style as "hard" or "soft"?

Hard schools of martial arts are those that emphasize proper positioning of the body, correct technique, muscular power, speed, and linear movement. Many northern Chinese styles of fighting are described as hard. Soft styles stress proper mental attitude, breath control, poise, form, balance, circular movement, and the development of internal energy, or ch'i. Whereas hard styles develop the strength of certain parts of the body to deliver more power, soft styles develop power from within that can be sent throughout the body where needed for effective defense. Soft styles emphasize maintaining good health, both internally and externally, to resist disease. Practitioners of soft martial arts often use an attacker's own momentum and power to defeat him or her. This kind of subtle manipulation of an aggressor calls for high standards of mental awareness and proper use of body mechanics.

In general, martial-arts forms are neither purely soft nor purely hard, but rather a blend of both. Even within a style there will be differences in emphasis, depending upon the teacher or what must be accomplished in a physical confrontation. Just as opposing forces of yin and yang reside in everything, hard and soft elements are both found in various styles of martial arts.

5. Do martial art students follow any particular code or set of regulations?

Many schools of martial arts teach

philosophy and ethics as part of their regular training. Many East Asian fighting forms base their teachings on concepts from the Tao, yin-yang, Chan Buddhism, and Confucianism. Individual styles of fighting may, however, set forth their own rules of conduct. There may even be differences among schools within the same style, based upon a particular teacher's thinking and goals. Beginning students must accept the regulations of their martial-arts school and strive to honor the regulations in all their actions. Below is a sample set of rules of conduct for a particular school of kempo:

- Practitioners must be sincere with themselves and others.
- Practitioners must dedicate themselves to continual improvement.
- Practitioners must show courtesy and respect toward all people, especially teachers and elders.
- Practitioners must be friendly, kind, honest, and fair with all people.
- In traveling, practitioners should refrain from showing off their fighting skills to others. Fighting techniques must be used

only for actual self-defense.

• Practitioners must exercise moderation in all they do.

• Practitioners must refrain from bragging or attempting to conquer.

• Practitioners must act in accordance with nature and its ways. They must strive to be in harmony with other people and the world around them.

6. Are there any general health secrets to be learned from Asian martial arts?

You can learn a great deal from the Asian martial arts to improve your health. Below is a set of suggestions to improve your health and make your training more effective:

• Avoid worrying, since anxiety can wear you out. If you can, do something immediately about any problem. When you take action, it will help dissolve fear, worry, and anxiety.

• Eat lightly so as not to overburden the body. Refrain from eating at least an hour before starting to train. Be sure your body receives proper nutrition, and avoid desserts and junk food.

• Drink an adequate amount of water daily. Water lubricates your system, clears your skin, and energizes you.

• Avoid doing anything, including martial arts, to excess. Practice moderation in all you do. Be patient yet persistent in achieving a goal. Do not expect immediate success or results. Instead, enjoy what you are doing and take life one day at a time.

• Exercise at least three times a week, and walk as much as you can. Use walking as a warm-up for training, a general body conditioner, and a natural relaxant. Make sure that any exercise program includes slow stretches, strength-building exercises, and endurance training.

• Practice proper body posture in everyday living as well as in the martial arts.

• In performing warm-up exercises, do not bounce, put excessive pressure on your joints, overbend a joint, or perform any movement too fast.

• Get sufficient sleep. This will keep your muscles rested, loose, and pliable.

• Use meditation as a tool to cut down on worry and anxiety.

• Set aside times to be alone and relax.

CHAPTER
5

PHYSICAL CONDITIONING

The human body was meant for action. Early humans had to use their bodies throughout the day to search for food and defend against attacks from animals or from other humans. In modern society, however, most people get little physical exercise. For that reason, if you are interested in starting martial-arts training, you should have a thorough medical examination to see if your body can handle rigorous study of an Asian fighting art.

If you are not in excellent condition, then you should discuss with your doctor what exercises would be appropriate for you to practice before beginning training. Preconditioning the body gives you a foundation of physical fitness so you can run less risk of injury when you first start martial-arts training. Any preconditioning program should include a balance of slow stretches, strength-building exercises, and endurance builders.

If you have your doctor's approval, and you are either in excellent condition or have completed a preconditioning program, you may start to work on the exercises taught in this chapter.

When performing these exercises, you should work within the limits of your own body. Exercise should help stretch, strengthen, and build coordination, but not cause you pain or injury. You should begin each training session with a brief walk, if possible, to warm up the body. Then proceed with a set of stretches, taking care not to bounce. Do all stretches and strength-building exercises very slowly at first so that you do not put more pressure on the body than it can handle.

Try to relax while performing exercises, and you will feel the gentle, pleasant sensation of your muscle stretching to release tension. You may have to hold a particular stretch for five seconds or more for the appropriate tension release. Allow the natural pull of gravity to help you stretch. Even in performing strengthening exercises, it is important to proceed slowly and with a continuous motion so the muscle can be built up throughout the movement. If you feel pain, you should immediately stop performing the exercise. Don't believe the old saying "no pain, no gain." If you persist in exercising even though you are experiencing pain, you run the risk of damaging your body.

You should perform slow conditioning exercises before and after training. In order to achieve proper health benefits, perform a full set of exercises at least three to four times a week. If you exercise two consecutive days, you should alternate activities. For example, on the first day, follow your initial stretching exercises with weight lifting to build your upper body. On the second day, work on your lower body by walking or bicycling.

A good conditioning program pursued over time will bring you many rewards: more energy, greater resistance to illness, greater ability to handle stress, release from anxiety, less chance of injury in sports, stronger bones, more efficient heart and lungs, better self-image, more self-confidence, and better performance of self-defense techniques. The key to achieving all this is making your exercise program a part of your regular daily living. The exercises that follow can be used for a partial foundation of any conditioning program.

Neck Stretches

Stand with your back straight and your knees slightly bent. Slowly lower your chin as far toward your chest as it will go without being forced. Bring your head back to the starting point. Perform the stretch five times. Turn your head slowly to the right, as far as feels comfortable, as if you were trying to look over that shoulder. Perform the stretch five times, and then do the same stretch to the left five times.

Looking straight ahead, lean your head to the right, so that your ear approaches your shoulder. Again, do not force the stretch. Remain relaxed and let gravity do the pulling. Perform the stretch five times. Then do the same stretch five times to the left. After doing these neck stretches for several weeks, you may add additional neck strengtheners.

further strengthen your neck as you move it from side to side. Place your hand on the right side of your head to offer slight resistance as you lower your head toward your shoulder. Perform the same movement on the left side. Remember, never push hard against your head or neck in performing these exercises.

Neck Strengtheners

After completing a set of neck-stretching exercises, place your hands against your forehead while your neck is in a natural stationary position. Gently push your head down toward your chest, as your hands slightly resist this motion. Do not push too hard. Allow your chin to move down straight against the gentle pressure of your hands. The goal is to build strength, not to cause pain and injury. This exercise can be modified to

Curl Down

On an exercise mat, lie down with your knees up and your feet resting flat. Bring your chin gently toward your chest. Next, fold your arms across your chest and bring your shoulders forward as you press your lower back against the mat. As your body curls forward, hold your stomach in and keep your lower back on the mat. Keep your knees bent, but allow your feet to shift slightly. Next, uncurl until your shoulders rest on the mat. Go slowly. At the beginning, take at least five seconds to curl up and five seconds to uncurl. Perform five times.

Basic Forward Stretch

Standing with your knees slightly bent, bring your arms up over your head. Keep your elbows slightly bent. Slowly reach toward the floor, but stretch only as far as you can go without discomfort. It is not necessary to actually touch the floor. When you reach your lowest point, hold that position for a count of at least five seconds. Then with your knees slightly bent, slowly return to an upright position.

24

Inner-Thigh Stretch

Sit on the mat with your back nearly straight and your knees bent. Place your hands on your lower legs, and place the bottoms of your feet together. Allow your right knee to tip naturally toward the floor and hold this position for a count of 10 before you return to the starting position. Next, do the same with your left knee. You will feel some stretching in your upper inner thigh, but don't force your knees to go lower than is natural and comfortable.

With your legs in the starting position (with your knees apart and the bottoms of your feet together), place your hands on your ankles. Pull your body forward, slowly and gently, so that your head approaches your feet. Keep your elbows out to the side and bend forward from the lower part of the body, not from the upper shoulders or waist. Hold your bent-forward position for at least five seconds and then slowly sit back up. Do not push too hard. Allow your body to move naturally and comfortably.

Lower-Leg Stretch

Place the palms of your hands against a wall or person, take one full step backward with one foot, and bring the other foot back to join it. Adjust your body until you feel a gentle stretching action from the calf of the leg downward, and hold the position for a count of 10. Then step forward and remove your hands from the wall or person.

Push-ups

The push-up is an excellent way to build upper-body strength. To perform it, lie face down on the mat, place the palms of your hands against the ground (with your fingers spread wide for stability), and place your feet two to four inches apart. Make sure that your knees are relaxed and slightly bent. With your weight on your palms and your toes, bring your body upward until your arms are nearly straight. Then bring your body down until your chest is just short of touching the ground. Perform five times.

Falling Exercises

Once you start training, you will have to learn a special type of exercise to protect your body when you are thrown to the ground. Falling exercises must be practiced very slowly on a safety mat designed for martial-arts use. At first, only practice falling exercises with the approval and direct supervision of a qualified martial-arts instructor. DO NOT allow anyone to throw you until you have developed excellent falling skills.

Rear Fall

You can use this falling technique if you are thrown backward or lose your balance and fall to the rear. Begin in a squatting position with your knees slightly bent. Tuck in your chin and extend your arms directly in front of you. Spring up with your knees and allow your body to fall backward. As you fall backward, extend your arms out to either side of your body. Just before your back hits the mat, break your fall by slapping your forearms down against the mat about six inches from either side of your body. Your head should not touch the mat at any point during the fall.

Side Fall

This is one of the most frequently used falling techniques. It is especially effective when you are thrown over an opponent's hip, shoulder, or leg. Begin in a squatting position with one leg crossed in front of the other. Keep your chin tucked down so that your head never hits the mat. Gradually slide your front leg forward so that you lose balance and fall on your side. While falling, raise the arm on the side of your body that will hit the mat. Just before you hit the mat, slap the palm of your raised hand against the mat to break your fall. Your body must land properly, so that the knees, ankles, and other sensitive spots are not hurt. Make sure that after you land, your body is in the position illustrated.

Front Fall

The front fall is effective when someone tackles, sweeps, or throws you forward. It can also be used at any time you slip and fall forward. Begin in a kneeling position on the mat. Rise up and let your body fall forward. Bring your arms up, palms facing the mat. Slap the mat with the palms of both hands to break your fall. Your head and stomach should not touch the mat at any point. Your hands and arms must remain stationary after they slap the mat so they can support your body and keep it from hitting the mat.

Meditation

The Eastern Warriors exercised both the mind and body. Meditation is a key form of mental exercise that can prepare you for martial-arts training and also help you handle the pressures of daily life. It can clear the mind, relax the body, and make you feel more receptive to learning. You can use meditation any time you want to relax. There is nothing supernatural in meditation, so don't expect anything more than a gentle feeling of relaxation. The following suggestions should be employed to start meditation:

Sit cross-legged on the floor with your hands in your lap. Hold your left thumb gently in your right hand. Keep your upper body erect and relaxed. At first, keep your eyes half open and concentrate on a spot directly in front of you; later you may close your eyes. Let your body go loose. Inhale deeply and hold your breath for a count of four, and then exhale through your mouth. Perform at least five times.

If you still feel tense after this deep-breathing exercise, tense your toes for a count of two and then release the tension. Imagine a gentle, relaxing heaviness flowing upward from your toes. As the heaviness moves upward, each part of your body should feel heavy, relaxed, and at ease. Visualize three successive waves of heaviness. After completing the three waves, close your eyes and visualize a time or place when you felt calm and content. Whenever your mind wanders, simply bring it back to this tranquil scene.

To come out of meditation, open your eyes gradually. Gently allow your body to return to its normal state. When you stand up, your mind and body will be relaxed and ready to handle the challenges of training or everyday living.

CHAPTER

6

FIGHTING POSTURES AND MOVEMENT

Any posture that you use in the martial arts is called a stance. Your fighting stance affects your stability and mobility, the type of tactics you use, and the amount of power you can put into fighting techniques. Beginning martial artists should carefully learn the basic stances and practice them until they become second nature. Your goal is to develop the ability to move in and out of the different stances in a smooth, effective manner to take advantage of their respective strengths.

You may have to adjust your stance quickly to use the technique that best meets the challenges of the situation. For example, when throwing kicks, you may want to move your feet closer together to shorten your stance. With your feet close together and your knees only slightly bent, you can move very quickly. At other times, you may want to increase the distance between your legs, even though you cannot move quickly when you are in this stance. In assuming a stance, you must not go too far in either direction. During a confrontation, you should maintain a proper stance, even when moving. This will increase your stability and make you better able to handle a charging adversary.

FIGHTING POSTURES

Natural Stance

The natural stance is used when you are at attention, beginning to take one of the other stances, or employing a defense that starts from a normal standing position. It can also be used to initiate certain throwing or holding techniques. Because of its adaptability, you should practice the natural stance and then learn how to move quickly from it to any other stance. This ability will enable you to take a strong and stable position if an attack is launched while you are standing in a natural manner.

To assume the natural stance, begin by facing your opponent with your feet two to six inches (5 to 15 cm) apart. Relax your shoulders and let your arms rest comfortably at your sides. Keep your back straight and your eyes focused directly in front of you.

To assume a right natural stance, begin in the basic natural stance and simply place your right foot forward. For a left natural stance, move your left foot forward from the basic natural stance. In any natural stance, keep your upper body face-forward and your weight evenly distributed over your feet.

Iron Horse Stance

This versatile stance can be used for either defense or attack and is especially useful for throwing powerful hand attacks. To assume the stance, start in the basic natural stance and step off to the side so that your feet are far apart—approximately two shoulder widths. Your upper body should be erect and your weight evenly distributed over your feet. Form fists with your hands and hold them palms up, slightly above the hips. (This hand position is used when practicing the stance, but in actual combat or sparring, one of the other hand-guard positions described later in this chapter would be more normal.)

The iron horse stance has two main variations—the diagonal stance and the side-facing horse stance. To assume a side-facing horse stance, simply step forward into a horse stance so that the side of your body faces the aggressor. To assume a diagonal horse stance, step to the front and side so that your body faces the aggressor at an angle.

Begin your training by practicing the traditional iron horse stance with a broad base. You can practice adjusting the stance to suit certain techniques later.

Bow Stance

This stance is very effective for attacking, and it can be used for defense as well. Begin in a basic natural stance. Step forward and to the side two shoulder widths with your left foot. Bend the forward leg and let it carry 60 percent of your body weight. Your rear leg should be nearly straight, with only a slight bend at the knee, and the heel of your rear leg should be flat against the ground. Turn your torso toward the opponent.

Your hands can be held in any of the hand-guard positions discussed later in this chapter. (The basic low-guard position is shown in the illustration.) The forward hand is commonly used for lead-in techniques to create openings for powerful attacks thrown from the rear.

The bow stance can be very useful in launching powerful punching techniques while maintaining a stable position. Throwing kicks from this stance is difficult, however, because of the foot placement and weight distribution.

Each variation of the iron horse stance has its advantages. The basic horse stance is excellent for practicing certain blocks and for launching powerful hand techniques. The side-facing horse stance makes you a more difficult target and is excellent for throwing side kicks. The diagonal horse stance gives you a stable base for defense and for launching powerful hand attacks.

All of the iron horse stances, however, lack flexibility and might make it difficult for you to move quickly and efficiently. Also, some kicking techniques may be difficult to execute from either the side-facing horse stance or the diagonal horse stance. If you put your feet a bit closer together, you could more easily throw certain kicks, but this would reduce your stability—and stability is one of the main reasons to assume this stance in the first place.

When using any of the iron horse stances, position your feet according to the fighting techniques needed at that particular time.

Cat Stance

The cat stance is a very effective position for certain defensive actions. From the basic natural stance, move your left foot forward so that it rests just in front of your rear leg with the ball of your foot on the ground. (The hands are formed like claws in the illustration.) Ninety percent of your weight should rest on your rear leg. This allows your front foot to move quickly for defensive kicking, which, when you time it properly, can effectively keep an aggressor at bay.

The cat stance, however, offers less flexibility for other fighting techniques. Because most of your weight is on your rear leg, you cannot easily throw kicks with that leg. Also, because the feet are so close together, you lack the stability needed for throwing powerful punches. Use the cat stance sparingly—mostly for defense and only when you want to operate from a narrow base.

Back Stance

The back stance is an excellent defensive position. To assume it, place one leg in front of the other. If you want a lot of mobility, place your feet approximately one and a half shoulder widths apart; if you want more stability, make it two shoulder widths. Deeply bend the rear leg and shift about 70 percent of your body weight onto it. The forward leg should be slightly bent. (The hands can be held in several positions. The full-guard hand position is illustrated.)

This stance is great for defending your front against an aggressor who is close or is lunging at you. It is stable, so it is good for blocking. In addition, since very little weight rests on the front leg, you can kick easily with this leg. This stance is not preferred, however, for moving forward with long-range hand or foot attacks or for initiating holds or throws. Choose the back stance as a defensive stance against an aggressor who is very near you or as an intermediate position when you shift attacks from long range to close range.

HAND-GUARD POSITIONS

Full-Guard Hand Position

This hand position allows you to guard against attacks to the upper body. It is also excellent for throwing open-hand blows or for grabbing. To take the full-guard hand position, open both hands. In most stances you will naturally place one arm farther forward than the other, but if your stance is one such as a front-facing horse stance, you may choose which arm will be your forward arm. The fingers on each hand should be pressed together and slightly downward with the thumb bent over so it is pressed against the palm. Your forward arm should be bent at the elbow, and your hand, palm facing out, should be in front of the body at slightly above shoulder level.

Position your rear arm across your midsection so that your rear hand, palm out, is at about the center of your torso. Both arms should be curved, but loose, so you can respond quickly. Concentrate on sending power to the bottom edge of your forward hand and the heel of your rear hand. The full-guard hand position can be used from any of the fighting stances.

Mid-Guard Hand Position

To take the mid-guard position, hold both hands open, palms out, at approximately chest level. (This hand position can also work well with one or both hands made into fists.) Your elbows should be pointed in toward the ribs. The mid-guard position allows you to follow up blocks with powerful rear punches and lets you move quickly to protect either your head or lower body.

As a variation, keep the forward arm slightly lower (at hip level) while the rear arm remains at a middle level. In this position, the forward arm can easily block low attacks, while the rear arm blocks blows at the chest and higher levels. In a confrontation, you may choose to change your hand position to distract your opponent, but be careful in doing so. Unless you concentrate on what you are doing and take quick action, your opponent may hit you while you are changing positions.

33

Low-Guard Hand Position

To take a low-guard position, hold your hands in fists at approximately hip level and protect your ribs by holding your elbows against them. If you want to grab an opponent quickly, tilt both of your open hands slightly upward. This guard lets you protect the groin and lower abdomen while keeping your hands in a position from which you can throw very quick punches or grab your opponent from close range.

To learn how to change hand positions effectively, assume each position from the different stances. Then practice switching from one hand position to the next, until you have used all of them while in each stance. Finally, practice changing hand-guard positions while moving from one stance to another.

MOVEMENT

Movement is an important tool for self-defense. Simply shifting from one stance to another is a subtle movement, but it can be an effective dodge or even a way of putting an aggressor off balance. While you are in a stable stance but have the ability to move quickly in any direction, your actions are unpredictable and you are flexible in your choice of techniques. You can avoid an attack, come close enough to counterattack, or move away to retreat.

By contrast, when you anchor yourself in one place, you are a steady target. To learn mobility, set up a stationary object (such as a punching bag) and practice moving straight in and out, in a circle, or at an angle to the object. Maintain proper balance throughout.

Single Step

With this move, you can go from a basic natural stance to a right natural stance or to a diagonal horse stance. It can also be used to move slightly backward or forward. To use this move in going from the natural stance to a diagonal horse stance, simply step forward and to the side with your left foot. Make

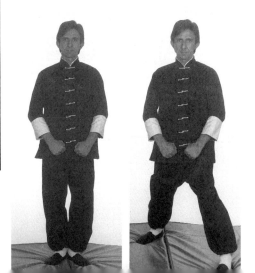

sure to end up with your knees bent and your torso positioned at an angle to the aggressor. You should maintain proper balance as you step and keep your body erect.

Slide Step

This technique allows you to keep the same foot in front of you as you move forward. It can be done from any of the fighting stances. If you start from the basic iron horse stance, you must first take a single step to get one foot out in front of the other. If you start from a diagonal horse stance, slide your front foot forward with a single step. Next, slide your back foot forward until you have regained your original stance. Be sure to maintain proper balance as you move. To move backward, slide your back foot to the rear and then follow with your front foot.

Circle Step

This step allows you to move around to an opponent's side or back. It is most often done from a diagonal horse stance or bow stance. From one of those stances, move the forward foot eight inches to the right or left, depending on which direction you want to go. Once the forward foot has moved, use it as a pivot to swing the rest of your body in the desired direction. After pivoting, make sure the rear foot is planted firmly on the ground again so you are in a strong fighting stance again. The model in this illustration is moving to his right. To move to the left, he would have stepped to the left with his forward foot and used that foot to pivot the rest of his body.

Side Step

To side step, consider the direction you're moving toward to avoid an attack. If you want to move to the left, simply take a step to the side with your left foot and then slide your right foot toward it. When side stepping to the right, step first with the right foot, and then move your left foot toward it, maintaining the proper distance for a strong, balanced stance.

EVASION MOVEMENT

Drop Dodge

When an aggressor moves forward to execute a blow, you may drop your body below the attack by bending your knees. This technique should be used only for attacks thrown at shoulder level or above. Keep your hands up for protection. In doing the drop dodge, you can also bend your knees and lower your upper body to the front or to the side. This type of dodge is usually used to evade a blow and begin a takedown or counterattack.

Stepping-to-the-Side Dodge

This dodge is also used for attacks at shoulder level or above. When an aggressor releases a blow, step off to the side as you bend your upper body away from the blow. One arm should be up, palm facing out, and ready to block, while the other hand is in a position to block or counterattack as needed.

Shift Dodge

This evasion can be performed any time you change from one stance to another or shift your body to change weight distribution in a stance. It is usually performed to avoid contact at shoulder level or above. From the basic iron horse stance, for example, transfer the majority of your weight to one of your legs, as the top half of your body bends toward that leg. Your hands should be positioned as shown in the illustration. The hand closest to the attacking limb can be used to counterattack or block, with the other hand positioned to block if needed.

Backward Dodge

This dodge can be used to avoid both punches and kicks at chest level or above. From the natural stance, step backward with one foot when your opponent launches a blow. At the same time, bend your upper body backward and transfer your weight to the rear bent leg. The front leg should still be bent at the knee. Once the aggressor's blow fails, spring forward and stand erect to execute a counterattack.

You can also use the backward dodge from a diagonal horse stance if you bend your rear leg deeply and transfer weight to it as your front leg straightens out. Be sure to keep your hands in a protective position for blocking, as shown in the illustration.

Once an attacker is off balance, you can also perform a takedown. Sometimes just moving unexpectedly to the side of an aggressor may throw him or her off balance. At other times, you may need to use the balance-disrupting tactics that follow.

Push-Pull

To unbalance an aggressor, you can use a simple push-pull method. When an attacker pushes you backward, pull him or her toward you. If an aggressor pulls you forward, push him or her away. In both cases, you are using the aggressor's force against him or her.

MOVEMENTS TO DISRUPT BALANCE

You can use your body movement to throw an aggressor off balance and leave him or her unable to oppose your counterattacks.

Pivot Movement

Pivoting is another method for disrupting an attacker's balance. Pivot movements use the aggressor's momentum against him or her. Pivoting can be done in one of two ways, depending on whether your opponent pushes or pulls you.

If an aggressor pushes you, pivot on one foot while you swing the other one around. As you pivot, pull in the direction that your opponent is pushing toward. If you are pulled forward, continue moving in the direction in which your opponent is pulling. You can do this by pivoting on one foot while swinging your other foot forward and to the side. As you pivot, push in the direction the aggressor is pulling you toward. These unbalancing techniques allow you to use an aggressor's upper-body movement to your advantage.

CHAPTER
7
SENSITIVE AREAS ON THE BODY

Besides their fighting skills, Eastern Warriors also have an understanding of the human body. This knowledge keeps them healthy and helps them defend against attacks. Just hitting an aggressor is not enough. An Eastern Warrior knows how to direct energy to strike key places on an opponent's body to discourage further aggression. Knowledge and finesse are two important characteristics of the Eastern Warrior. A fighter can sometimes discourage further aggression simply by pushing on or hitting sensitive areas of the body.

The two diagrams show sensitive areas of the body for simple self-defense.

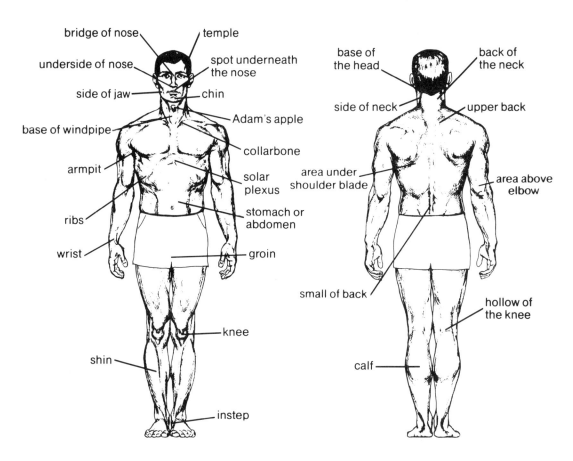

CHAPTER
8

SAFETY-RANGE AND LONG-RANGE DEFENSES

Training as an Eastern Warrior gives you the ability to monitor a situation properly, so that you can avoid—if possible—a physical confrontation. If a fight must take place, then you should be able to defend yourself. To best understand how to protect yourself, you should first keep in mind that attacks are launched from different distances. Inexperienced people are often caught off guard by an attack because they do not understand the three ranges of distance: safety range, long range, and close range.

Safety range is the distance at which your adversary cannot reach you with a blow. Similarly, your blows cannot reach your opponent. Long range is the distance at which either you or your opponent can hit the other with certain hand or foot attacks, such as a front kick or left jab. At close range, you and your aggressor are near enough to hit each other with punches, knees, or elbows. From this distance, either you or an aggressor may also move to apply a hold or execute a throw.

It is important to think in terms of these ranges and plan your strategy accordingly. For example, if your aggressor is the type who would throw a sucker punch, you may want to at first stand in safety range. If you are an excellent wrestler, you may choose to

stand near enough so that you can carefully thwart the attack and then use your strong grappling techniques to end the confrontation.

In the course of a prolonged fight, you may move in and out of the three ranges while defending yourself and executing counterattacks. This chapter shows you how to defend yourself and counterattack from the various ranges of distance.

In a real confrontation, you will have to defend and counterattack smoothly and efficiently. Because a skilled aggressor may rapidly follow one punch with another, block-

43

ing alone won't adequately protect you. You should follow an aggressor's attack with your own blow to a sensitive or weak area. If your first blow does not stop the aggression, follow through with a series of blows. To be effective, an Eastern Warrior must learn to put together combinations of techniques. To develop a tight defense against aggression, be observant. Adapt the techniques shown here (and others you may learn) to the needs of the situation.

NOTE: Although both people in this chapter's illustrations start out with their left foot forward (unless otherwise stated in the text), you should practice the various techniques from both sides of the body. That practice will help you respond appropriately to any variation in your adversary's aggression.

BASIC WAYS TO DEFEND AGAINST ATTACKS FROM SAFETY-RANGE AND LONG-RANGE DISTANCES

You may respond to a long-range attack by evading, parrying, or blocking, and then counterattacking. Make sure you do not respond mechanically. Carefully judge your distance from an adversary as he or she attacks, and time your defense to make it effective.

In the following illustrated lessons, an aggressor initially attacks from safety range or long range. During the fight, however, the defender must protect and counterattack from close range as well. Similarly, in a real physical confrontation you should expect different attacks from various ranges.

Evasion, Block, and Counterattack against a Side Kick

If your opponent starts in safety range and begins to move forward quickly, assume a strong fighting stance, such as the side-facing horse stance. You should expect a side kick if the opponent turns his or her body to the side and lifts the front leg, but you can evade the kick.

If you are in a side-facing horse stance with your left foot forward, transfer your weight to your right rear leg as you begin to pivot on it. Swing your left leg around behind you until you end up in a side-facing horse stance out of the line of fire of your attacker's kicking leg. As you are shifting your body, bring your right arm up so that, if necessary, you can block the kicking leg with a forearm block. Once the kicking leg has been evaded or deflected, slide step forward and counterattack with a right backfist strike to your opponent's head. Follow up by stepping off to the side with your left foot as you execute a left punch to the opponent's body.

If you are in a fighting stance with your hands in a full-guard position, a scissors block can be effective against a side kick thrown very quickly at your stomach. As the kick is launched, bring your forward arm down in a bent position. Your rear arm also should be bent across your stomach. Once the opponent's leg comes near your hands, close the trap by snapping the lower arm up while sweeping the upper arm down and to the side. The opponent's foot is caught between your left and right arms, and the kick is neutralized. You can then push the attacking limb away or grab the aggressor's foot and execute your own front kick.

Block and Takedown against a Long-Range Front Kick

If an opponent starts out in safety range and moves closer, quickly assume a strong fighting position such as the diagonal horse stance. If the aggressor's rear foot moves, he or she might be preparing to throw a front kick. Bring your arms down so that they cross and meet, ready to block the attacker's kick between them before it hits your body. Once you have stopped the kick, grab the leg with both hands and lift it until the opponent falls to the floor.

Checking a Kick with the Foot

If you are in safety range and an opponent quickly moves nearer into long range, assume a narrow diagonal horse stance so your rear leg can execute a quick kick. As your opponent moves his or her leg to execute a kick, bend your rear leg at the knee and bring it up. Thrust your leg out so that the bottom of your foot hits the opponent's foot, ankle, or shin to check the kick before it can be launched.

Evasion, Block, and Counterattack against a Roundhouse Kick

When an opponent puts weight on the forward leg and starts to lift his or her rear leg up and to the side, prepare to be dealt a roundhouse kick.

The moment you sense an opponent's aggression, assume a strong fighting stance such as one of the horse stances. Once the opponent's rear leg starts to lift for a roundhouse kick, pivot on your front leg as you swing your rear leg to the side and farther behind you. The front of your body will be out of the direct line of force from your opponent's blow. At the same time, bring up your forward arm so that it blocks the opponent's kicking leg. Your opponent may try to punch you with his or her right arm, but you can use your forward arm to block this attack as well. To counterattack, step off and to the side with your front foot. Then slide step toward the aggressor as you begin to shoot straight out with a right punch off the rear side to your opponent's body or head.

Countering a Grab

When you are standing in a natural stance and an aggressor begins to charge from long range to grab you, step forward with your left foot into a diagonal horse stance. At the same time, parry your opponent's grabbing arms outward with the palms of your hands.

Once the attacking arms have been deflected, make your right hand into a fist and drive it straight into the opponent's abdomen. Follow up by snapping your left hand outward, with the palm open and facing out, so that the soft bottom edge of it hits the side of the attacker's neck.

Defense against a Powerful Right Swing Punch

An aggressor may charge you while throwing a wild, swinging punch with his or her right hand (especially if your adversary is right-handed). This type of opponent is used to ending a fight quickly by raining blows upon an unsuspecting person. If you are in a natural stance, pivot on your right foot and turn your left side to face the aggressor. Bend your left (forward) leg at the knee and lift it in a coiled position with your knee off to the side. Shoot your leg out with a side kick so that the heel of your foot hits the aggressor's knees, groin, or abdomen. Put your left foot down.

If you sense further aggression, move forward and snap your left arm outward to hit your opponent's upper body with a punch from your forward hand. If necessary, continue to defend by stepping off to the right with your right foot as you turn your rear hip forward and execute a right punch to the opponent's midsection or chest.

Counter from a Basic Natural Stance for a Right Step-in Swing Punch

If an aggressor is at long range and moves the right rear foot forward while beginning to throw a swing punch off the same side, evade the blow by stepping to your left side with the left foot. At the same time, block your attacker's right punch by bringing your left arm up to meet and deflect the attacking arm. Follow up by making your right hand into a fist while you move closer to the attacker. Extend the middle finger of your fist and drive it up into the aggressor's solar plexus. (See diagram, p. 42.) Your left hand should now be in an open-hand position with the thumb folded over, as it drives down to strike the opponent's neck.

Defense and Takedown from the Rear against a Right Lunge Punch

If you are in a basic natural stance and an opponent steps forward with the right rear foot to throw a straight punch with the right arm, step to the left with your right foot. Once you are out of the way of the attacking lunge punch, bring up the back of your right forearm to deflect the opponent's blow. Step forward with your left foot as your right hand executes a short vertical punch to the side of the attacker's head. Then reach out with your right hand and grab the opponent by either the back of the collar or the hair. At the same time, lift your right leg off the ground with the knee bent, and thrust this leg out so that you hit the opponent behind the right knee. As you kick, pull back against the aggressor's hair or collar to throw the aggressor down against the ground.

Countering a Right Lunge Punch from a Side-facing Horse Stance

If an adversary has an extremely powerful right-hand punch, you may have to grab that hand as soon as possible to keep your opponent from using it against you. When an aggressor steps forward with a right punch and you are in a side-facing horse stance, step to your left. Parry the blow with your left hand. Follow up by making your right hand into a fist and turning your arm so that your knuckles are pointing up when you hit the opponent's ribs. Next, bring your right arm up quickly to grab the opponent's right arm. Turn your left hip forward and shoot your left arm out with a turning action so that your fist hits the opponent's head. Now, slide to your opponent's rear as you grab his or her right shoulder with your left hand. Finish by turning your body and bringing your leg up to sweep the opponent's right foot off the ground.

Countering a Right Lunge Punch from a Diagonal Horse Stance

If you are in a stable stance with your left foot forward, and an opponent moves to perform a right lunge punch, you can try to cut off the attack by slipping behind the attacker. To start, step to the side with your left foot as the aggressor moves forward to throw a punch. Put the fingers of your right hand together and fold your thumb over. The soft bottom edge of your right hand should catch the attacker's right attacking arm on the outside and deflect it toward his or her chest. Move your left foot behind the attacker as you lower your right arm and snap it out to hit the aggressor in the midsection with the bony edge of your hand just below the thumb. Grab the opponent with your right hand to contain further aggression. Pivot on your left foot and bring your right foot around so that you are almost directly behind the aggressor.

If necessary, finish your counterattack by punching the attacker with your left hand. In practice, never actually make contact with a sensitive area on your partner's body.

DEFENSES AGAINST A LEFT JAB

One of the more common techniques in long-range fighting is the left jab. You will find it thrown as a lead technique to keep you at bay, as a setup for other blows, or as part of a combination of techniques. You must learn to defend against it in a number of ways.

Parry and Combination Counter for a Left Jab

If an opponent moves forward quickly with a left jab, assume a strong fighting stance, such as a left-facing diagonal horse stance. As the left hand moves toward you, parry the blow in and down with your own forward left hand so that the force is neutralized. Transfer weight to your forward leg as you twist your right (rear) hip forward. Turn your right fist and strike so that the knuckles are up when you hit the opponent's chin. Next, pivot on your left foot, bringing your left arm around with a circular motion so that your left hand—which is open with the fingers placed tightly together and thumb folded over—snaps inward to the side of the opponent's neck. The bony edge just below your thumb should hit the opponent's neck in what is called a ridge-hand blow. Follow up, if necessary, with a close, palm-up punch to the opponent's body.

Evasion, Parry, and Counterattack against a Mid-Level Jab

If an opponent moves forward with a mid-level left jab, it might be difficult to execute a drop dodge. Instead, you can evade the blow and end up alongside the aggressor, where you are less vulnerable to attack. This type of maneuver also allows you to execute a blow, hold, or throw. From this position, you can hit parts of your opponent's body that he or she will not be able to protect with a block.

If you are in a natural stance and an opponent executes a left jab, step forward into a diagonal horse stance with your right foot to your opponent's left. At the same time, move your right palm out to parry the opponent's left jab. After your right hand has neutralized the blow, pivot sharply at the waist and drive your left hand up and under the opponent's guard with a punch to the mid-level of the opponent. Next, twist your right hip toward the opponent and launch a circular punch so that the thumb side of your right fist is up when it hits the side of the opponent's jaw. At the same time, slip your left hand up and behind the opponent's left arm to grab it.

Dodge and Counterattack against Charge with Left Jab

If the opponent charges in very quickly with a left jab, step forward and to the left about eight inches with your forward (left) foot. Shifting the majority of your weight to your left leg, drop below the attacker's guard by bending your knees down and lowering the top half of your torso in a drop dodge. Your left hand should be held high, ready to protect against any right punch from your opponent. Drive outward with your own right punch to the ribs or abdomen. This defense can catch an opponent off guard with a very powerful punch.

Defending against a One-Two Punch Combination

Sometimes when you are in a fighting stance, an opponent may move in with a quick series of punches. When the first is a fast jab with his or her forward arm, the second punch, with his or her rear arm, will have more power because of the body weight behind it. This combination is called a one-two punch. When you are in a strong stance and your opponent throws a left jab at your face, bring your right hand up and deflect the blow with your palm. Use the palm of your left (forward) hand to deflect the opponent's second right straight punch.

BLOCKING AND COUNTERING WITH THE SAME HAND

Sometimes you will want to move very quickly to stop an attacker's blow, thus preserving your energy and catching your opponent off guard. You can do this by using hand movements that both block and counterattack with the same arm.

Handling a Left Jab with a Right Block and Circle Punch

If an aggressor throws a left jab, bring your right hip toward him or her. At the same time, bring your right forearm up under the opponent's blow to deflect it outward. Keep your left hand in front of your body for added protection. Once the blow has been neutralized, bring your right elbow up in line with your opponent's chin. Shift your weight to the left leg as you execute a right circle punch to the opponent's head. Follow up by twisting your left side to the right and driving your left fist into the opponent's stomach.

Deflect and Counter with the Right Hand against a Left Swing Punch

If an opponent moves forward with a wide-swinging left-arm punch, step to the left and shift your weight in that direction. Turn your right hip to the left as you drive your right arm out to deflect the opponent's blow before it reaches you. Once the attacking limb is stopped, your right hand should be formed into a fist and shot straight through to hit the opponent's chin. Your right hand has not only blocked the opponent's swinging punch but has ended up as a counterattack. You may follow with an additional counterattack by sliding forward with your left foot and delivering a left punch to the opponent's head.

Brush-away Palm Block and Backfist Counter for a Palm-up Punch

If an opponent moves forward with the right hand to deliver a palm-up punch, quickly lower your open left hand to brush the blow down and away. Once the blow has been neutralized, make your left hand into a fist and snap it upward. Your backfist strike should hit the opponent's face. You may follow through by executing an additional right punch to the chest.

leg as you drive a hard left palm-up punch into the opponent's chin.

Lower-Arm Block and Ridge-Hand Blow against a Left Jab

If an opponent moves forward to execute a left jab, raise your right forearm to intercept the blow from the inside and deflect it. Your right hand should be open with the fingers pressed together and the thumb folded over. Once you have blocked the blow with your right forearm, transfer weight to your left leg and raise your right elbow to shoulder level. Snap your right arm inward to deliver a ridge-hand blow to the side of the opponent's neck. You may follow up by pivoting on your left

59

Palm Parry and Open-Hand Blow against a Left Jab

If an opponent moves forward with a left jab toward your chin, reach across with the palm of your left open hand to parry the opponent's blow. After you have parried the left blow, bend your thumb over and slide forward. Snap your left arm out at the elbow so that the soft bottom edge of your hand hits the side of the opponent's neck. Follow through with an additional counterattack, if necessary, by turning your right hip forward and executing a palm-up punch to the opponent's midsection.

Forearm Block, Backfist Strike, Elbow Blow, and Sweep against a Backfist Strike

If an opponent in a right forward stance snaps a right backfist strike, shift from a natural stance to a left side-facing horse stance. Execute a left inward forearm block to deflect the attacker's right backfist strike. Turn your body into your block so that you sweep the aggressor's arm inward. Once the blow has been blocked, grab the attacker's right arm with your left hand. Recoil your left arm and execute a backfist strike to the attacker's face. Then move forward with an elbow attack to your opponent's upper body. As soon as you have delivered the two blows, grab the aggressor with your left hand and sweep his or her right (forward) leg off the ground with your leg.

Block and Backfist Strike with the Same Hand

If an opponent attacks with a right punch, deflect it inward with a left mid-level forearm block. Quickly reach over with your right hand and grab the attacker's right arm. Your block should have diverted the attacker's momentum, giving you time to bring your left blocking arm back near your ear in a fist, thumb side up. Snap this left fist out and catch the opponent off guard with a backfist strike to the face.

CLOSING AN OPPONENT'S CENTERLINE AND COUNTERATTACKING

Imagine a line running vertically along the center of your body. You will find that many sensitive areas fall very close to this line. It is important to defend this vital area against attack, while increasing your ability to hit the opponent's sensitive areas. One very effective way of doing this is by closing the opponent's centerline. This is done by drawing one of the opponent's limbs across to the other side of his or her body with a block, parry, or grab. This tactic turns the opponent's body away from you, and from that position, he or she cannot bring much power to bear against you. Your tactics should involve three stages: an initial stop of the attack, the actual turning of the opponent away from you, and your counterattack blow.

Once the opponent's limb has been swept across to the other side, that person will be turned away from you and will be off balance. When two skilled fighters are up against one another, the one who performs this maneuver first usually wins.

Basic Parry, Sweep, and Counterattack

If an opponent throws a left jab, parry it with your left palm. Aim for the outside of the

attacker's arm, pushing it inward. Next, rotate your left arm so that your arm and your opponent's punching arm are back to back, and continue to sweep the attacking limb across the aggressor's centerline so that you turn him or her away from you. Lastly, follow through with a right punch to the aggressor's body. This three-step maneuver enables you to defend, turn the opponent away, and execute your own counterattack.

Parry, Block with Other Arm, and Counterattack

If an opponent throws a right-hand blow, use the palm of your left hand to parry the blow inward. Once the blow has been neutralized, sweep the outside of your attacker's arm with your right arm and continue to sweep it across the opponent's body, turning the opponent away from you. Follow with a left punch to the opponent's body.

When an opponent executes a left jab, parry it inward with your right hand. Once you have halted the blow, use a left outward forearm block to continue to take the attacking arm toward and across the opponent's body. Follow by counterattacking with your right hand to the opponent's body.

TRAPPING AN OPPONENT

When an aggressor moves near enough to hit you with long or short punches or to grab you, the conflict is on the border between long range and close range. If you wanted to define the combat range a little better, you could move either closer to or farther from your opponent. You can, however, stay at this distance and trap your opponent's hands while you finish the fight with your blows.

Most trapping movements start when an opponent blocks one of your blows or hand movements. The first step in trapping is to acquire skill in grabbing and neutralizing an opponent's limbs. You must be able to perform the movements smoothly, efficiently, quickly, and with the correct timing. This skill can only be developed by prolonged practice with a partner. At first, such techniques should only be practiced under the supervision of a qualified instructor.

Check Forward Hand and Follow-through Punch

When you are facing off against an aggressor who is nearly toe-to-toe with you in a fighting stance, you may be able to end the fight with a simple trap. Quickly lower your left (forward) hand on your opponent's left (forward) fist to tie it up. Once you have a hold, quickly move forward and release a right-hand punch to the aggressor's face.

Catch Block and Follow-up

One way to trap an opponent is by capturing an attacking limb with a catch block. When you are squared off against an opponent and he or she executes a right straight punch in close, bring your bent left arm up to intercept the attacker's blow with a forearm block. Next, turn your left palm downward as you lower the attacker's limb. Slide your left hand down the attacker's arm to grab his or her wrist. Follow up by counterattacking with a right-hand punch.

Straight-Arm Lock Trap for a Right Punch

When you are in a natural stance and an aggressor moves forward with a right lunge punch, step into a horse stance. Bring your right hand up with a mid-level forearm block that meets the attacking limb at the elbow. After your arm starts to deflect the blow, quickly bring up your other arm to grab the attacker's punching arm. Your right hand should grab the attacker's right wrist. Press down with your right hand on the attacker's wrist as your left hand pushes down on his or her elbow to trap him or her in a straight-arm lock. You may follow up by bringing your knee up to hit the aggressor.

Trapping an Opponent Who Uses a Downward Push Block

If you attempt to throw a left punch and your opponent blocks it by pushing downward with his or her right arm, reach down and grab your opponent's right wrist with your right hand. Bring the captured right wrist down while aiming your left fist at the opponent's face. If the opponent's left arm comes up to block your fist, bring your left hand around and grab the blocking arm by the wrist. Bring your opponent's left arm across the body so that it wraps over his or her right arm. This will allow you to trap both of the opponent's arms by using only your left arm. Since you no longer need to grip your opponent with your right hand, you can follow through with a right-hand punch to the opponent's head.

Setting Up a Trap with a Left Lead

If you are in a left forward stance, your adversary has the same side forward, and there is a brief pause in the conflict, you may want to take positive action to end the aggression. Jab with your left (forward) hand at the opponent's face as you grab and neutralize his or her left arm with your right hand. If your opponent blocks your left punch with his or her right free arm, grab the blocking hand at the wrist with your left hand and bring it down so that it is even with the opponent's left hand. Swiftly bring your right arm over his or her left, so that your right hand grabs the opponent's right wrist. At the same time, release the grip that you have with your left hand. Finish the action by driving your left fist to the opponent's head as your right hand pulls on the opponent's right wrist to turn him or her away.

Trapping an Opponent's Block and Parry

If you are in close and your opponent attempts to block your left punch with a left hand, grab his or her left blocking arm at the wrist with your left hand. Bring the blocking arm down as you punch with your right (rear)

70

arm. Should your opponent attempt to parry your blow with his or her right hand, slightly retract your punching arm and press your right palm down on the free hand that deflected your blow. Your right palm should continue to push your opponent's right hand down until it rests against his or her left arm. Quickly grasp the opponent's right hand with your left so that both arms are tied up while you drive your right fist out underneath his or her chin.

Trapping an Opponent Who Blocks a Left Backfist Strike

If an opponent blocks your left backfist strike with a left forearm block, immediately follow up by grabbing the opponent's blocking arm with your striking hand to pull it downward. At the same time, throw a right punch toward your opponent's head. Should the opponent move to block your second blow with his or her right arm, immediately grab his or her right wrist. Pull it down across the opponent's body so that his or her right arm is pulled over the left and entangled with it. You may follow through with a left-hand punch. This technique is useful when you are up against an aggressor who continually blocks and grabs during your counterattack.

9

CLOSE-RANGE DEFENSES

Generally, when your opponent executes a straight punch, swinging punch, far-reaching hand strike, or kick where the limb is nearly fully extended, it is described as a long-range attack. In contrast, when your opponent executes a circular punch, elbow strike, uppercut, short-reaching hand strike, or knee kick—or when he or she grabs you from quite near with a deeply bent limb—it is a close-range attack.

This distinction, however, is not always clear. Sometimes an aggressor at close range will be able to deliver a blow, such as a jab or vertical punch, that is normally delivered from long range. The blow may not, however, have the desired snap or power because it cannot gather momentum. This chapter will first deal with defenses against blows that come from the borderline region between long and close range. It will then introduce defenses for blows thrown from very close range. The next chapter will describe close-range maneuvers of a different type—grappling and wrestling techniques.

Defense against a Left Vertical Punch

If an aggressor leads with a left vertical punch, dodge it by bending the top half of your body forward to the inside. Grab the hollow of the opponent's left knee with both hands while bringing your head close to his

or her chest. Step forward with your right leg as you straighten up and lift the opponent's left leg off the ground. Next, step forward with your left leg and hook it behind the aggressor's right (rear) leg, sweeping it out from underneath him or her as you direct your weight forward.

Dodge and Takedown against a Left Swing Punch

When you are in a natural stance and an aggressor steps forward with a left swing punch, step off to your right with the right foot while bending down and away to avoid the blow. Move in very close to the aggressor to gain leverage for the takedown that follows. Keep your chin tucked and your left hand ready to block, while you reach down from the outside with your right hand to the hollow of the aggressor's left forward knee. Next, pull with your right hand and push back on the aggressor's chest with your left while shifting your weight forward. This technique can be used anytime an aggressor leads with a left blow while he or she is near enough for you to grab the legs as required.

finish with a right palm-up punch to the mid-level of the body, followed by a left punch to the chin.

Stamp Kick against a Left Swing Punch

When an opponent throws a left swing punch while standing directly in front of you with his or her lead foot next to yours, you are on the border between long and close range. When the attack is launched, sweep the left punch away with a block with your right arm and then grab the punching arm with your right hand. While your right hand grasps the attacker's left arm, grab his or her right arm with your left hand. Follow up by lifting your right knee and stamping down on the aggressor's left shin and foot. You may

Defending against a Right Swing Punch and Knee Kick Combination

When you are nearly toe-to-toe with an opponent and he or she throws a right swing punch, use your left palm to parry the attacking arm. If the opponent moves in with a second attack by driving the left knee up toward your groin, bring the palm of your right hand down to deflect the knee. Follow through by making your right hand into a fist and punching, palm up, into the attacker's abdomen. You may then follow through with an additional left-fist blow. Transfer weight onto your left front leg, and with the thumb side of your fist facing up, hit your opponent in the head with a left circle punch.

Dodge and Takedown against a Vertical Punch

When you are in a natural stance and an aggressor moves in close to throw a left vertical punch, immediately step forward with your left leg and bend your upper body down and to your left to avoid the blow. Grab the opponent's left (forward) leg behind the knee from the outside with your right hand. At the same time, slip your left hand between the opponent's legs and grab the right leg at the hollow of the knee. Tucking in your chin for safety, press your head against your opponent's body. Turn your body to the right as you pull the captured legs up and toward you so the aggressor is thrown to the ground. This same maneuver can also be used when you are in a left forward stance and an aggressor executes a left straight punch.

Block against Choking Attack with Knee Kick Counter

If you are in a basic natural stance and an opponent reaches out to choke you, step forward with your left foot into a diagonal horse stance. Lower your knees into a solid stance while bringing your arms in between the attacker's grasping limbs. Sweep your arms out and then downward, so the attacking limbs are thrown off to the side. Follow by grabbing the opponent's arms and driving your own right knee up and into the opponent's groin.

Dodge and Takedown against a Grabbing Attack from in Close

When an aggressor moves in close to perform a grabbing action against you while you are in a natural stance, step forward and to the side with your left leg. At the same time, bend down to avoid your opponent's grabbing hands and grasp his or her forward leg behind the knee with both hands. Move in close and place your head against the aggressor's body with your chin tucked to protect against attack. Straighten up and lift your opponent's left (front) leg off the ground. Then step forward with your left leg and hook it behind the opponent's right supporting leg, sweeping it out from under him or her.

Blocking a Right Vertical Punch in Close

If you are squared off in close with an attacker who throws a right vertical punch, lower your body and turn your head to your right side. Place your right arm, palm out, in front of your face to block the blow if necessary. Once you have evaded the attacker's blow, follow through with a left palm-up punch to the mid-level of the attacker's body. Next, reach up with your left hand and grab the opponent's left arm, pulling it down and away. At the same time, come up and pivot on your left foot as you deliver a right circle punch.

Dodge and Takedown against a Right Vertical Lunge Punch

If an aggressor steps forward with the right foot while executing a right vertical punch, bend your upper body forward and to your right to evade the blow. Place your head as close as possible to the opponent's body, keeping your chin tucked in for safety. At the same time, swing your left arm around the opponent's waist. Bend your knees deeply and move your right hand down from the inside to grab the hollow of the opponent's right (forward) knee. Straighten your body while pulling upward with your right hand and back with your left so that the aggressor is lifted off the ground. Then bend forward and throw him or her to the ground.

Check, Stamp, and Punch

When you are faced off in close against an aggressor who throws a kick at your shins or knees, bring your left leg up, bending at the knee, and stamp down on the opponent's kicking leg. Follow up, if necessary, by stamping on his or her left foot as well. At the same time, put your left (forward) hand over the opponent's right arm to keep him or her from throwing any punches. Quickly bring your right hand down onto the opponent's lead arm as you make your forward left hand into a fist and hit the opponent's chin. This fast series of movements will slow the aggressor so that you can try to end the fight with a blow.

82

Block, Grab, and Takedown against a Left Circle Punch

If an aggressor moves to throw a left circle punch, raise both of your forearms so they intercept and deflect the blow. Grab the attacking arm with your right hand as you step forward with your left leg, placing yourself behind the opponent's left (forward) leg. Quickly grab the aggressor's shoulder with your left hand, push backward, and sweep your opponent's front leg out from underneath him or her with your left leg.

Defense and Takedown against a Right Lunge Punch

If you are in a left-facing stance and an aggressor lunges forward with a right punch, execute a left forearm block to intercept the blow from the inside and push it outward. After you have completed your block, retract your left (blocking) arm and drop your body down forward and low. Hit your opponent in the hip with a right palm-heel punch while you grab his or her forward leg behind the heel with your left hand. Pull the aggressor's right heel out so that he or she is thrown to the ground.

CHAPTER

10

GRAPPLING AND WRESTLING

When an opponent believes that you are physically weaker, he or she may try to wrestle you into submission or grapple with you on the ground. You must learn how to handle this type of aggression and how to avoid panicking when an aggressor grabs you or throws you.

This chapter deals first with defenses to use against grabbing attacks when you and the aggressor are standing. Defensive moves and escapes for grappling on the ground are also covered.

Learn the techniques in this chapter step by step before actually trying to practice them. Next, perform the techniques very slowly with a partner and under the super-

vision of a qualified instructor. Remain loose and do not exert yourself any more than necessary. If you try too hard and become stiff, you will lose the natural, coordinated effort needed to succeed.

For safety reasons, do not exert real force against a partner when practicing escapes. Pay constant attention to what you are doing and release any holds or pressure the moment you sense that your partner is feeling any discomfort. You and your partner should work out a signal—a tap on the arm, a stamp of the foot, some simple word like "okay"— to indicate that a hold or another action should stop immediately.

Do not ever try to perform escapes or

other similar grappling maneuvers until your body is thoroughly warmed up. Make sure that you are comfortable with the steps throughout the movement before doing it. Never allow anyone to practice a hold on you unless you are familiar with the moves, understand where the pressure will be applied, and are properly supervised. Your goal is to become more effective in self-defense, not to prove how tough you are in practice. Show kindness and consideration to other people in practice and do everything possible to avoid injury.

DEFENSES AGAINST GRABBING ATTACKS

To defend against grabbing attacks when you and your opponent are standing, observe carefully what your opponent is trying to do and take appropriate action. Your moves should have a purpose; don't just struggle aimlessly or attempt to break an aggressor's hold with muscle. Instead, use psychology and knowledge of the human body to force a release of the hold. Sometimes all you need is to distract the aggressor momentarily to pull out of the hold. At other times, you may need to put pressure on a vulnerable spot by, for example, bending back a finger or striking at your opponent's centerline. You may have to perform a number of moves in combination to get out of the aggressor's grasp. If you remain calm throughout and use good judgment, you should be able to extract yourself from even the most difficult physical confrontation.

Release from a Wrist Grab

If an aggressor grabs your wrist, pull your arm out at the weakest point of his or her grip, which is where the thumb meets the fingers. Adjust your arm movement to escape, depending upon the actual grip on your arm. The same principle—putting pressure on the thumb—can allow you to escape from many different holds.

Release from a Double Hand Grip

If an aggressor grabs both of your wrists, escape by rotating your arms to weaken the grip. Then snap both wrists outward against the aggressor's gripping thumbs. You may want to first pull one wrist out of the aggressor's grip, and then the other, or pull both hands out at once, depending on what seems most likely to be effective.

Release from an Upper-Arm Grab

When you are in close, an aggressor may grab your upper arm to start a clinching action. This is often done to intimidate you or to stop you from executing any punches. It can even be the first move in an attempt to wrestle you to the ground. To escape, make the hand on your gripped arm into a fist while bringing that arm up and out with a circular action directed against the aggressor's thumb.

Release from a Single-Arm Grip from Behind

If an aggressor grabs your upper arm from behind, turn and step toward him or her. To free the arm, make that hand into a fist and bring your arm up and nearly straight out toward the aggressor. Continue moving your arm up and to the side until you have freed it. Keep your hands ready to block further attacks.

Release from a Double Grip from Behind

If an opponent grabs both of your upper arms from behind, first step forward with your left foot while you twist your body to the right and toward your opponent. Sweep your right arm up and under the opponent's lower right wrist to knock his or her grip loose. Then step forward on your right foot and walk away. If your opponent is able to maintain a hold, bring your right leg up into a coiled position with your toes pointed upward and kick back against the opponent's body to force a release of the hold.

small fingers of your opponent's hands. Pull the fingers out to put pressure on them.

Release from a Choking Maneuver

If an opponent chokes you from the front or behind with both hands, stiffen your neck while bringing your hands up to grab the

Release from a Hair Grip

If an aggressor grabs you by the hair from the front, place one of your hands, palm down, hard upon the gripping hand. Then place your other hand on top. Hold firmly as you step forward and apply downward pressure on the aggressor's hand and wrist, while continually bending forward.

If an aggressor grabs your hair from behind, place one palm firmly against the back of the aggressor's hand and place your other hand on top of it. The downward pressure of your hands should counteract the pull on your hair. Turn your body to the side and circle under the aggressor's grabbing arm to bend the captured wrist backward. Once you are facing your opponent, continue to push back and up to put added pressure on his or her wrist. Continue applying force until you break free.

GRAPPLING ON THE GROUND

If you are thrown to the ground, you must protect against further aggression. Do not despair. Seize the advantage by keeping a clear mind and setting up a series of moves. This strategy will allow you to move from one technique to the next until you achieve your goal.

Whenever you are forced down with your back against the ground, keep both legs bent at the knee. Your bent legs may act as a barrier against an adversary. Kick any aggressor foolish enough to move in to attack. Even if your opponent is too close for you to execute a kick, you can still use your legs to push him or her away. Try to keep space between your body and the aggressor's.

If your opponent starts to apply a hold or to pin you, use all of your body for defense. You will often be able to escape by using a flowing action from one side of the body to the other. Keep your whole body moving so that your adversary cannot perform a finishing act. You should not, however, move too quickly or without purpose. Instead, try to get in a position to either counterattack from the ground or from a standing position again.

When fighting on the ground, use your shoulders and body when pushing or pulling with your arms. You will have maximum leverage and force if you push at one spot. Even if an opponent gets on top, you can still escape by taking advantage of his or her weakness. Coordinated moves with your arms, hips, and legs usually will help you escape. You can dislodge your adversary by shifting your weight enough to weaken one side and put him or her off balance. Move

quickly to exploit that weakness by slipping away. If you cannot move to a standing position, then defend yourself by applying a hold. Once you apply a hold on an opponent, you must remain close to maintain control of his or her body, keeping your body low with your knee against your opponent's side. If your adversary begins to move away, slide your knee into him or her to retain control.

In the process of grappling, you should not take any unnecessary risk by jumping directly on an adversary. This can be dangerous and leave you open to attack. Instead, move in cautiously to gain control of the part of your opponent's body that you will use to accomplish your goal. If possible, pin down the opponent's arms and legs so that he or she cannot hit you. Do not merely defend your position while on the ground; use every opportunity to seize control of the situation by hitting your opponent in sensitive areas, applying a lock, or moving free of his or her grasp.

Takedown from a Grounded Position in Front of an Aggressor

If in the midst of a fight you are forced to your knees in front of the aggressor, quickly reach your right arm behind his or her forward knee, sweeping your left arm across the aggressor's body. Next, pull hard on the opponent's knee as your left arm pushes him or her to the ground.

Defense against a Kick While on the Ground

If in the midst of a fight you are forced to the ground and an opponent starts to throw a kick, bring your forward arm up by your face, bending deeply at the elbow. Sweep your arm down and across the opponent's kicking leg to deflect it. If your opponent continues to move toward you, retract your elbow and then snap it out so that the bottom of your fist hits the aggressor in the groin with a hammer blow.

If your opponent continues to be aggressive after you complete your block, follow through with a far-reaching counterattack. Fall to the floor with your hands supporting you. Bring one leg up toward your chest with the knee deeply bent. Thrust the leg out so that your foot hits the aggressor's body. Immediately retract your leg to prepare for an additional kick.

Takedown against a Standing Aggressor

When you have been forced to the ground and the aggressor is at your side, turn your body so that your chest faces your opponent's side. At the same time, grab his or her closer leg above the ankle with one hand. With your other hand, grab the same leg a little higher, around the calf. Lift the aggressor's leg as you begin to stand. Keep your chin safely tucked. Once your body is nearly erect, take your hand from around the aggressor's calf and drive it, palm outward, against your opponent's chest. At the same time, continue to lift behind the opponent's ankle and drive forward to throw him or her backward to the ground.

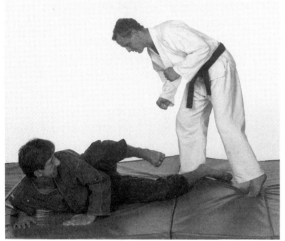

Defense against a Front Kick While Beginning to Stand

If you are beginning to stand up and an aggressor throws a front kick, cross your arms down on his or her leg, catching it between your arms. Grab the attacking limb with your hands. Once you are erect, keep lifting the captured limb and position your body so that one of your legs is behind the aggressor's supporting leg. Sweep the supporting leg outward so he or she is forced to the ground. When practicing this and all throws and takedowns, DO NOT finish this takedown by actually performing the sweep, but simulate the action to familiarize yourself with the process.

Release from a Hair Grip from the Front

If an aggressor grabs your hair with the left hand to pull you down, bring your right hand under his or her elbow while your left hand grips the wrist of the attacking arm. At the same time, rise up and turn your body to the right, toward the outside of the attacking arm. Lift up on the aggressor's arm and turn it while bending his or her wrist back with your left hand. Now push down on the elbow while continuing to press back on the wrist so that the aggressor is in a combination arm lock and wrist lock.

Escape from a Grabbing Attack

If you are forced to face an aggressor from the ground, and he or she grabs you with the left hand while preparing to punch you with the right, grab the gripping arm at the elbow with your right hand and at the wrist with your left. At the same time, turn your body so that it is outside the aggressor's left arm. Quickly bend his or her wrist back with your left hand while pushing down on the elbow with your right.

Escape from a Choke

When an opponent faces you on the ground and starts to choke you, reach over with both hands to pry his or her right hand away. Turn the captured wrist so the palm faces the opponent. If you have difficulty, simply bend back the aggressor's smallest finger to force a release. With a firm wrist lock, keep turning the captured hand to the outside past the aggressor's front. This should break the choke hold while containing further aggression. In practice sessions, DO NOT actually apply pressure to your partner's wrist. Gently simulate the movement.

Defense against a Grip from the Rear

When an aggressor tries to grab you by slipping his or her left arm underneath your left arm from the rear, pull your left arm tightly to your body to pin the attacking arm. Quickly turn your left side to the right as you lower your body, tuck your chin, and roll over, throwing the attacker down on his or her back. Finish by delivering a rear elbow strike.

Escape from an Opponent's Grab from the Side

If you are on your knees and an aggressor reaches around your body with his or her right arm, bring your closest arm around to pin the aggressor's grabbing arm close to your body. At the same time, turn your knees toward your opponent, bring your shoulder down, and roll your body so that the aggressor is thrown on his or her back. Finish with an elbow strike.

Defense When Choked from the Side

If you are on your back and an aggressor chokes you from the side, bring your closest knee (the right in the illustration) up to the aggressor's midsection. Swing your other leg up so that the back of your knee moves around your opponent's head. At the same time, grab the aggressor's left arm with both hands and pull it straight. Drive your left leg down so the opponent's head and body are brought down with it. With your hand, quickly grip your opponent's right arm as you pull it, palm up, across your lower body in a straight-arm bar with pressure on his or her elbow.

Defense against a Forearm Choke

When an aggressor straddles you and presses his or her forearm on your throat as you lie on the ground, reach up with your left hand and grab your opponent's hair or ear on the left side. Use your grip to pull him or her to your left as you turn your body sideways and push with your right hand to throw the aggressor off of you. Finish the escape with an open-hand blow with your right hand.

Defense against a Punch When Your Back Is on the Ground

When your opponent is on top, with legs bent on either side and arm raised to throw a right punch, bring your left arm up to block the punch from the inside. At the same time, shoot your right arm across your body under the attacking limb. After the blow has been neutralized, grab the aggressor's right wrist with your left hand and pull down while bringing your right arm over to hook the aggressor's elbow. Turn the aggressor's right arm palm up and then apply pressure at the elbow. Use an arm bar to force your opponent face down to your right.

to pull your right arm free. Now use the right arm to deliver an elbow blow.

Escape from a Headlock on the Ground

If an aggressor has one arm around your neck and is holding on to your right arm, reach around with a free hand to pull your opponent's hair or ear. Use the action of your left hand as a distraction to allow you

CHAPTER
11
STRATEGY

Asian martial arts that are characterized as hard use some soft movements, while soft arts rely on hard movements at times. Many Eastern Warriors combine, consistently with the yin-yang concept, tactics from both soft and hard arts in developing an overall strategy. Likelihood of success in a battle can be increased by using a strategy that draws on the most effective tactics for any given situation. The following is a listing of basic strategic guidelines that include both hard and soft tactics. They should be learned, understood, and practiced in a manner consistent with the East Asian martial art that you are studying.

1. Keep presence of mind. Your greatest asset in any self-defense situation is your mind. Muscle power cannot substitute for proper thinking. For that reason, it is important that you keep your presence of mind, even when confronted by a dangerous opponent. One way you can do this is by breathing deeply while concentrating on your adversary. When you have your mind clear, you will be able to adapt to the needs of the situation, while focusing all of your power for self-defense.

2. Think and act confidently. If you believe you can do something, you have usually won half the battle. In any confrontation against an opponent or otherwise, the greatest psychological barrier to success that you will have will be the one you place in front of you. Once a physical confrontation begins, you must assume that you can overcome your opponent.

   Do not concern yourself with whether you believe your opponent is more skillful, powerful, or a better fighter than you. Instead, simply clear your mind and form a strategy while allowing your body to spontaneously execute the techniques that you have learned through practice.

   You should show confidence in the way you execute movement and techniques. Avoid moving away from your opponent when delivering a punch because it may lack power and give an indication of fear. Timidity only serves to encourage a bully to believe that he or she will overcome you, and it lessens your ability to use proper strategy in the use of techniques.

   Seize the psychological advantage by taking charge of what takes place in the fight. Once the battle has begun, survival may depend on strategically setting the adversary up for your victory. If you are hit by that person, do not show that you are hurt. Make your adversary think his or her best blow will not affect you. Don't forget that your adversary, in a prolonged confrontation, will be just as tired and afraid as you are. The person that shows confidence throughout will have the psychological edge. Never allow yourself to get disheartened or discouraged. All it may take to turn the tide of battle in your favor or even to win is to land one good blow on a sensitive area of an adversary.

3. Make strategic plans. Use your mind to outthink the opponent and catch him or her off guard with tactical maneuvers. Once the fight begins, keep moving while you form a strategic plan. You should monitor your opponent's performance to judge strengths and weaknesses. Fight the kind of battle that you think that person most fears. While forming your strategy you should pay particular attention to the kind of movements the opponent does before throwing a lead technique or making an aggressive movement. Note any peculiarities in the opponent's techniques or the openings that person may leave. Form a strategy that takes advantage of what you have observed.

4. Protect your centerline. Since the centerline of vital spots applies to both the front and back of the body, you must take appropriate measures to avoid being hit either on the front or back along the centerline. Any attack or defense should take serious consideration of both the centerline of your body and the centerline of an adversary. If you have to expose part of your body, that part should be outside of the centerline.

5. Take advantage of body position. Assume the appropriate fighting stance for a particular confrontation. Judge your opponent's stance and attack whatever weaknesses are in it. You may also take advantage of that person's body position while moving if there are any weaknesses in balance. In a confrontation, you will need to constantly analyze your opponent's body position, your own position, and what actions are necessary for you to exploit the situation in a way that will end the fight. Just moving in at a particular angle may offer a terrific opportunity to take advantage of a weakness in an opponent's body position. Even the smallest of flaws can be exploited if you use your head.

Below is a list of rules for you to follow in making sure your own body position is properly used.

• When attacking, it is safest to come in

- When attacking, it is safest to come in from the side or rear rather than forward in a direct line.
- In throwing a punch, do not take an overly wide stance, since you may lose full rotation of the hips, and the ability to move quickly and execute certain kicking maneuvers. Do not, however, stand with your feet too close together, because your balance may be weakened and you may not be able to deliver a powerful punch.
- In executing a blow, always use your weight to add force. If you are moving backward, stop momentarily and then execute your blow. Once you have finished the technique, you can keep moving back. When executing a blow, concentrate on hitting through the target, not just hitting the surface. This will make your technique substantially more powerful and effective.
- Learn to shift body positions quickly so that you can switch from defensive action to offensive action when needed. Proper use of body position throughout a fight will ensure greater likelihood of success, even against a more powerful opponent.

6. Use techniques efficiently and effectively. In a real confrontation, it is always best to avoid a blow by evading it. If you cannot dodge the blow, then at least use a parry. A block can be executed if there is no better protection. The less contact you have with your opponent, the more energy you will be able to maintain for defense.

Think of self-defense as an organized process that allows you to effectively come up with a solution. Consider the three distances (safety range, long range, and close range) when determining what techniques you need at a particular point. You should learn to create openings for yourself by executing those techniques that will be most effective from a particular range.

Any consideration of distance must also involve timing as well. It will not help to execute a blow unless your timing is correct so that it hits the target at the proper distance.

Time your blows so that they hit openings on your opponent when that person is in a particular position at the correct range of distance. Carefully observe your opponent's posture to determine where that person will be most vulnerable to attack. If an opponent sees you punch toward the head, he or she will tend to lean away, so there may be an opening for another blow below the beltline. On the other hand, when a blow is thrown below the beltline, an opponent will tend to move backward while momentarily leaving the top half of the body leaning forward. At this time, an additional blow to the upper half of the body would probably be effective.

An opponent can sometimes be hit more easily when he or she is preparing to make a move. For that reason, you should carefully watch that person's movement and time your blows accordingly. It is also useful to move against an opponent if that person seems tense or distracted. Even a tough adversary will leave openings when shifting weight to change stance, moving hand positions, or reacting to your fake. In a fight, time your counterblow for the moment when the opponent leaves a clear opening, changes techniques, crosses from one range of distance to another, takes a break in movement and types of techniques, or momentarily ends his or her attack.

7. Exploit your adversary's weakness in balance. Continually monitor the opponent to check balance. Be sure to exploit the off-balance position of that person immediately. A blow that hits an off-balance opponent is far more likely to make

that person falter. When you effectively catch him or her with a blow, you gain a psychological edge, and possibly an opportunity to end the fight.

Be ready at all times for an opportunity to use the four methods of off-balancing taught earlier in this book. When these off-balancing movements are executed from close range, you may effectively take over control of the fight by your ability to take advantage of your opponent's movement. Watch the opponent while moving around in a prolonged confrontation. When he or she moves to change the lead side, there will be an opportunity for you to disrupt his or her balance. Another time to take advantage of poor balance is when an opponent stumbles or has assumed a narrow stance with a lack of stability. If you are observant, you will find numerous opportunities to exploit the opponent's balance to your advantage.

8. Use angular and circular movements for defense. If you are up against an aggressor who leaves the centerline open, you may choose to move straight forward to attack the sensitive areas. When retreating, however, it is best not to move straight back, but to move away at an angle. That way, you can make it more difficult for him or her to hit you.

Unless there are obvious openings at your opponent's centerline, you should use angular or circular movements. By placing your body at an angle, you put the opponent in a position where he or she may not easily hit you or put full power behind a punch. If you square off against your opponent and exchange blows, you face great danger. Fighting at an angle or moving behind him or her allows an escape from a dangerous predicament.

Do not forget that a parry, grab, or pull can also place you at an angle in the same way as evading with your legs.

9. Use combinations. A single blow to a sensitive area will sometimes stop an aggressor. You must, however, always have another technique ready in case the first blow does not end the fight. In certain situations, you may want your first blow to act as a distraction for a more powerful follow-up technique. For these reasons, it is important to link fighting techniques in combination. If a blow takes the fight out of an aggressor, then you do not need to use follow-up techniques, but it is important to have them available, if necessary, to continue to bring your battle to the opponent.

Speed, timing, and distance considerations all affect the effectiveness of a set of combinations. In order to properly penetrate the aggressor's guard, you will need to do more than simply throw a series of blows. You must first monitor the opponent's performance to look for patterns or openings that can be exploited. Once you have found those, you must time your combination of techniques so that they hit the opponent at just the right distance.

Repeat even the best of combinations sparingly. An adversary will take advantage of any knowledge of what you are going to do by counterattacking in the midst of your set of techniques. Any combination of movements that you use must flow in a continuous attack. Each blow should act as a setup for the next. It will do you very little good to simply throw out a series of fighting techniques in a mechanical way. Vary the rhythm of your blows. Do not telegraph to the opponent what to expect next.

10. Keep your opponent confused. An adversary who cannot focus his or her mind and skills fully on the fight will be far easier to handle. Take control of the situation by keeping that person confused.

This can sometimes be done by simply distracting him or her by yelling, throwing an object, or faking one attack as you launch another. Using fakes or distractions as setups for powerful blows greatly increases your chance of success in a fight.

11. Use efficient tactics to end a confrontation. When dealing with an aggressor, it is important to gauge his or her intentions, strength, skill, and ability to harm you from different ranges of distance. Choose techniques that will allow you to exploit weaknesses of an opponent. Avoid energy-wasting movements that do not move the fight toward an early end. Your footwork should be quick and

should not let your opponent know what you are going to do next. Remember, the most efficient way to end a fight is to choose the right tactics for a particular distance. When you are in safety range, you may avoid unexpected harm from a sucker punch, but do not expect to be able to continue to remain at that distance throughout a fight. It is likely that your opponent will be able to eventually move near enough to reach you with a blow.

Blocking a powerful opponent's blows may drain your energy. When your opponent is taller and stronger than you, it is often preferable to try to evade or at least parry his or her blows. The most efficient defense may be to defend and counterattack at the same time by evading or parrying while striking with your own blow. When you have to block, you may block and counterattack with the same arm. After deflecting your attacker's arm, your blocking limb moves to hit the opponent with a blow. Sometimes the quickest way to end a fight is to make an opening at the attacker's centerline by using blocking actions to sweep his or her arms away to the outside.

When you are unsure of whether you will be able to evade an attacker's harmful response to your attack, use blocks that close the opponent's centerline so that he or she cannot get at you with a counterattack. Your blocking arm deflects the opponent's arm across the other side of his or her body so that he or she has a difficult time executing another technique. When dealing with an aggressor who is skilled at blocking and counterattacking, take advantage of trapping techniques to tie him or her up. If executing blows against an aggressor does not appear to be the most efficient defense, then move quickly into close range where you can apply a lock or a takedown against an opponent.

12. Adapt your responses to the particular situation. You must remain flexible in your use of techniques for self-defense. Do not get into a habit of defending in a certain way against particular types of attacks. Instead, learn to respond according to each situation. The techniques of defense taught in the lessons of this book can easily be adapted to meet many different types of attacks. Practice putting together different combinations of the blows, escapes, holds, and throws that you have learned. In this way, you will be able to successfully defend against any bully's weaponless physical aggression. Keep in mind that each opponent that you face will have peculiarities, strengths, and weaknesses. Your ability to exploit any gaps in his or her defense while emphasizing your strengths will be the key to a successful result.

CHAPTER

12

SAFETY CONSIDERATIONS

In order to get the most out of your training, treat each practice session as an opportunity to learn, not as an opportunity to show your toughness and strength. If you remember that a practice session is not a real fight, you will enjoy your training more and avoid injuries. Training sessions should be used to broaden the mind, condition the body, build skill, and learn how to work with other people. To reach these objectives, follow these suggestions:

1. Keep in mind that you are studying martial arts for self-improvement. You do not have to show how tough you are to anybody in practice.
2. Only work out when you feel well and are not upset or tired. Your body must be loose, and you must have enough energy to perform the techniques properly.
3. Perform warm-up exercises and stretches before each training session. Make sure that you and your partner are thoroughly warmed up, well stretched, and loose before applying any holds or locking techniques. At the end of your practice, finish with a set of slow stretching exercises.
4. Don't be in a hurry to stretch your muscles. Be patient with your body and do not expect it to stretch out quickly. It may take months to get your body into condition when you first begin to train.

Practice an exercise or technique slowly and gradually over time. When you try to rush progress, the risk of injury increases.

5. Do not hit a partner while practicing punches or kicks. Stop all blows at least one inch from your partner's body. Do not even simulate blows to sensitive areas such as eyes, nose, throat, neck, ribs, groin, knees, or other areas along the centerline. Practice contact on a large punching bag. Only very advanced practitioners—under the supervision of a qualified instructor and in very limited circumstances—will actually hit a partner.

6. Never surprise your partner with a throw, sweep, or hold in practice. Be sure that your partner is ready to start before you execute these techniques. Become proficient at falling techniques before allowing anyone to throw you, and never throw a partner in practice unless he or she has excellent falling skills.

7. Work out a warning system with your partner to signal that a hold or lock is painful, so that it can be immediately released.

8. Practice holds, locks, throws, or grappling techniques only under the direct supervision of a qualified martial-arts instructor on a safety mat.

9. Wear proper safety equipment for your training exercise at all times. At a minimum, you should wear a headguard, a mouthpiece, a groin protector, and a set of knee pads in practice. When practicing punching and kicking techniques with a partner, in addition to full safety gear, always wear heavily cushioned gloves and safety shoes designed for use in martial arts. When you practice punches or kicks on a bag or other solid surface, wear protective gloves and safety shoes or boots.

10. Avoid the use of flashy techniques illustrated in the movies. Instead, practice the basics to develop a proper foundation of self-defense techniques.

Index

Art of War, The, 7

blocking and countering with the same hand, 57-62

centerline, 63, 102-103, 109
Chan Buddhism, 8, 14-15, 16, 19
ch'i, 9
Chuan-Fa, 6, 9-10
Ch'ueh Yuan, 9
close range, 43, 73
closing an opponent's centerline and counterattacking, 63-65
Confucianism, 13-14, 16, 19
curl down, 24

Daruma, 8
defense: from close range, 73-84; against grabbing attacks, 86-90; against a left jab, 54-56; from long range, 44-53; from safety range, 44-53
dodge: backward, 38; drop, 37, 55; shift, 38; stepping-to-the-side, 37

empty hand, 10
escape from: choke, 96; grabbing attack, 96; grab from the side, 98; headlock on the ground, 100
external boxing systems, 9

falling exercises, 26-27

grappling, 85-90; on the ground, 91-100

hand-guard positions: full-guard, 32, 33; low-guard, 31, 34; mid-guard, 33
hard martial arts style, 19

I Chin Ching, 9
internal boxing systems, 9, 10

ju-jutsu, 6, 10

Kalaripayit, 7
karate, 10, 18
kempo, 6, 10
Kung-Fu, 8, 9-10

Lao-Tzu, 11-12
long range, 43

meditation, 28
Muscle-Change Classic, 9

neck strengtheners, 23
no-mind, 15
northern school, 9-10, 18-19

pankration, 7
pivot movement, 40
pure mind, 14-15
push-pull, 39
push-ups, 26

release from: choking maneuver, 89; double grip from behind, 88; double hand grip, 87; hair grip, 90; hair grip from the front, 95; single-arm grip from behind, 88; upper-arm grab, 87; wrist grab, 86

safety range, 43
safety techniques, 109-110
sensitive areas on the body, 41-42
Shaolin temple, 8-9, 14
soft martial arts style, 19
southern school, 9-10, 18-19
stance, 29, 103-104; back, 32; bow, 31; cat, 32; diagonal, 30; horse, 30; iron horse, 30-31; natural, 30
step: circle, 35; side, 36; single, 34; slide, 35
strategy, 101-108
stretch: basic forward, 24; inner-thigh, 25; lower-leg, 25; neck, 22

Sun-Tzu, 7

takedown: and dodge against a left swing punch, 74; from a grounded position in front of an aggressor, 92; against a standing aggressor, 93
Ta Mo, 8-9, 14
Tao, 11-12, 16, 19
trapping an opponent, 66-72

visualization, 17

wrestling, 85-100

Yangtze River, 9, 12
yin-yang, 13, 16, 19

Zen Buddhism, 8, 14

About the Author

Fred Neff started his training in the Asian fighting arts at the age of eight. In 1974, Mr. Neff received a rank of fifth degree black belt in karate. The same year he was made a master of the art of kempo at a formal ceremony. He is also proficient in Chuan-Fa, judo, and jujutsu. Mr. Neff's study of East Asian culture has taken him to such lands as Hong Kong, Japan, the People's Republic of China, and Singapore.

For many years, Mr. Neff has used his knowledge to help and educate others. He has taught karate at the University of Minnesota, the University of Wisconsin, Hamline University and Inver Hills Community College in St. Paul, Minnesota. He has also organized and supervised self-defense classes for special education programs, public schools, private institutions, and city recreation departments. Included in his teaching program have been classes for law enforcement officers.

He has received many awards in recognition of his accomplishments and his active community involvement, including the City of St. Paul Citizen of the Month Award in 1975, a Commendation for Distinguished Service from the Sibley County Attorney's Office in 1980, the WCCO Radio Good Neighbor Award in 1985, the Lamp of Knowledge Award from the Twin Cities Lawyers Guild in 1986, and the Presidential medal of merit from President George Bush.

Fred Neff graduated with high distinction from the University of Minnesota College of

Education in 1970. In 1976, he received his J.D. degree from William Mitchell College of Law in St. Paul, Minnesota. Mr. Neff is a practicing attorney in Minneapolis, Minnesota.

He is the author of 19 books, including *Everybody's Book of Self-Defense, Lessons from the Western Warriors, Lessons from the Fighting Commandos, Lessons from the Japanese Masters* and the eight books that make up Fred Neff's Self-Defense Library.